D1823940

ALL YOU NEED TO KNOW (AND MORE) ABOUT THE 2018 WORLD CUP

Facts, Fun and Football

ALAN PETERS

About the Author

Alan Peters is a writer with a passion for sport. He publishes regular blogs and is frequently commissioned to offer his views on a number of sports related subjects.

These have included such various topics as sport and politics in Barcelona, the brilliance of Rod Laver, minority sports and sport and tensions in the Balkans. He has written about the history of rugby clubs to the trickery and tactics of Eton Fives.

His books include two novels – Blaize and Plague Boy - plus a travelogue on the Isles of Scilly: Britain's Most Amazing Islands. He has published three collections of plays.

All are available on Kindle or in Paperback through Amazon.

He lives in the Midlands with his wife, two children and dog. The wife and kids are not too interested in football, but he holds out hope for the dog.

Copyright © 2017.

All rights reserved. No part of this publication may be reproduced, distributed, or transmitted in any form or by any means, including photocopying, recording, or other electronic or mechanical methods, without the prior written permission of the publisher, except in the case of brief quotations embodied in critical reviews and certain other noncommercial uses permitted by copyright law.

This book is intended for informational and entertainment purposes only. The publisher limits all liability arising from this work to the fullest extent of the law.

Contents

Introduction

As we get older, the gap between World Cups seems to grow shorter. When researching this book, I started to check out the magnificent goal Michael Owen scored against Argentina.

That must have been about 2006, I thought, only to slowly realise that it had in fact been in the previous century.

But if one thing coming around more quickly is good news, then that event is the World Cup.

The 2018 competition promises to be one of the best ever. There are several teams in with a serious chance of victory.

Germany, Brazil, Argentina, Belgium, France – then who would rule out teams such as Uruguay or Spain?

Even England, we might hope with ever naïve optimism, might finally do something good at a major tournament.

But added to the general excitement is the fact that the finals are taking place in Russia. Will politics play an additional dimension? How will fans behave? Surely, none would risk the wrath of the Russian police forces? But then again, hooligans are not renowned for their sensible behaviour.

Written for publication immediately the draw is made, this will be one of the first books to offer a detailed and realistic look at the chances of teams as they attempt to win the 2018 World Cup.

England's Chances

Here we go again. The expectations begin to rise, the anticipation grows. Qualification has ended, the draw has been made; England has avoided the Group of Death, but the media will try to pretend otherwise.

Will England be able to put their stamp on the cup in Russia?

Those cheap flags of St George on plastic sticks that attach themselves to car windows are on order, accountants at Amazon and The Pound Shop are rubbing their hands with delight and Mrs. May is wondering whether the votes gained in England by appearing to support our lads will be more than those she loses in Wales, Scotland and Northern Ireland.

We are assured constantly that Gareth Southgate is going to give the youngsters a chance, or perhaps stick with experience, because you never win anything with kids. On the other hand, will he resign before the tournament having been tricked by a journalist dressed as Sepp Blatter into admitting that he thinks the ex-boss of Fifa is not as bad as he is made out? It is all so exciting.

And what of tactics? Apparently, Gareth will play 5-3-2 – definitely; unless it's 4-4-2…maybe in seeking out another grey FA suit, he will gain inspiration from his wardrobe and employ the coat hanger?

With such high-brow thoughts swirling like the ball on a wet night in St Petersburg, let us take a serious look at England's chances, it's history and the men who might just possibly forever embed themselves in the nation's consciousness next Summer.

World Cup Pedigree

1950 – Group Stage, second of four

1954 – Quarter finals

1958 – Group stage, third of four

1962 – Quarter finals

1966 – Winners

1970 – Quarter finals

1982 – Second group stage, second of three

1986 – Quarter finals

1990 – Fourth

1998 – Last sixteen

2002 – Quarter finals

2006 – Quarter finals

2010 – Last sixteen

2014 – Group stage, fourth of four

Star Player – John Stones

The Manchester City forward has come on leaps and bounds this season. The catastrophic and oh too regular mishaps that plagued his earlier career seem to be nightmares of the past, and his coolness on the ball is now of iced calm.

We have to be sensible here. There will not be many games, certainly from the knock out stages, where England will dominate possession. Therefore, they will need to hit on the break and build from the back. Stones is the man who can start such moves, more than any other English defender.

Yes, we will need the likes of Harry Kane, Dele Alli and our marauding wing backs, but Stones could become the key figure in the team.

Who Might We Know?

If there is a player in the squad that we don't know inside out by the time of the first match, then Southgate will have sprung a last-minute surprise.

Of more interest when it comes to England is who is not on the plane. Will Southgate have the belief to pick a squad capable of going far, playing exciting football but also at risk of messing things up? Or, and this seems more likely given his last few games, will he pick 23 Mr. Safes, the second eleven just slightly less good versions of the first? Will for example, the forwards include somebody who offers something different, like an Andy Carroll?

Will he be prepared to take a gamble on a midfielder who does more than run around energetically before losing the ball? Jack Wilshere comes to mind. Will he trust in players who have the extra qualities – pace, a trick or two – to win matches (Theo Walcott has never let England down, despite his limited opportunities), or will he count on not conceding many and hoping to score the odd one or two here or there?

Manager: Gareth Southgate

Mr. Southgate says the right things, and is unlikely to upset anybody important. He keeps telling us he is prepared to make tough calls, and to be fair, he did remove Wayne Rooney from the squad. But, like many before him, he seems obsessed with getting as many Spurs players in as possible and keeping the suits happy.

Perhaps a degree of 'playing the game' is the only way – look at how Sam Allardyce, a manager who would have got the very best out of the limited supply of players available, was abandoned so readily.

But, for all our doubts, we fans should get behind the coach, cross our fingers and hope for the best.

Road to the Finals

A comfortable process, with just the odd draw as a hiccup. But then, it is hard to think of an easier group to have been in. Slovakia, Scotland, Slovenia, Lithuania and Malta. Still, as the cliché goes, you can only beat what is in front of you...and yourself. We know that England are usually pretty good at qualifying, at least in recent years, but fall short when it comes to the real thing.

Prospects

England should be good enough to get out of the group stages, but beyond that, anything is a bonus. Most of the country would prefer to see a team that works hard but also has enough flair to give entertainment than a bunch of blind alley finders who quickly run out of steam, despite giving their all.

But there are some advantages for this tournament. Expectations are lower than ever, which might remove some of the pressure. Many of the squad (and Southgate could be clever here...) are not shoe ins for their club sides, so might be a little fresher than is normal.

The climate should suit England more than in many parts of the world.

We can but hope.

Player from the Past: Glenn Hoddle

The rumour is that Glenn Hoddle's party trick was to set four balls in the centre circle, and hit each one so that it landed on a different corner flag.

Such was his sublime touch that this writer can believe that the story is true.

As a very young and naïve journalist, your author interviewed a young Hoddle, who was making an impact for Spurs and England. The task was to compare two sports players from Harlow, the Essex town of Hoddle's upbringing. The comparison would be with a young schoolboy gymnast who had just won the national championships for his age group. Sadly, his name is now forgotten to all but his family, but if he is reading this book, I hope you remember the young man who took you out of your maths lesson for an interview, and that your sport has been good to you through your life.

Hoddle answered his own phone – I can't remember how I got his number – which really surprised me, and I recall a friendly, helpful guy who was brilliant until, about fifteen minutes in (I had not received an invitation to his house) he obviously got bored and directed me to his agent; this growling, vicious hyena made it totally clear that 'Mr. Hoddle is not giving interviews.'

And that was rather like Hoddle's career both as a player and a coach. Very promising, but ultimately failing to deliver all it offered.

In the playing sense, he can hardly be blamed. Hoddle made his England debut in 1979, and went on to earn 53 caps, scoring eight goals. As impressive as this sounds, it is not all that such a sublime passer, such a creative mind should have achieved. But Hoddle played in a time of shockingly poor pitches, when the extent of foreign influence was limited to players from Scotland and the odd Dutchman, and when hard graft, blind alley running and hard tackling were regarded more highly than exquisite skills.

His best international moments came in helping to guide England to the quarter finals of the 1986 World Cup finals; who knows, had Maradona not used his hand in that match, and England had progressed, perhaps Hoddle would be remembered as a great player, rather than as a very, very good one.

He was a successful manager as well, always ready to give youth a chance. Starting by reviving the fortunes of struggling Swindon Town, as player manager and not only saving them from relegation to the third tier, but earning them a place in the Premier league when they defeated Leicester City in the play-off final at Wembley. (Useful bit of trivia, Swindon did play in the Premier league, and were also promoted to the dying days of the old First Division, but were stripped of their promotion when financial irregularities came to light.)

He moved on to become player manager of Chelsea, and he got them to the final of the FA Cup and semi finals of the Cup Winners' Cup.

His next post was as England manager, and he showed much promise. But his inclusion of 'faith healer' Eileen Drewery among his back-room staff saw the press heap ridicule on his head.

Then, in an interview prior at the beginning of 1999, he made that fateful statement, which he insists was taken out of context. The journalist conducting the interview reported that Hoddle believed that disabled people were being punished for sins committed in a former life.

Harlow Technical College – the inspiration behind the author's interview with the great Glenn Hoddle – love the cars in the foreground

The thing about Britain is, free speech is completely permissible unless politicians feel that there are more votes in opposing it. Sports Minister Tony Banks and the then Prime Minister, Mr. Weapons of Mass Destruction Blair, pounced on the words, and grabbed an opportunity to win brownie points with the public.

The bandwagon gathered pace, and although Hoddle was almost certainly no more than naïve to utter his thoughts to a journalist, his England role was taken away from him. Things have clearly improved in the years up to Sam Allardyce's time as head coach!

Hoddle returned to club management with good, but not outstanding, success, then set up business interests and now is one of the more informed and considered pundits on TV.

Organisation of the tournament

It's a big country – who will conquer it?

Venues

With the venues located in the west of the country, travel times will be kept to a minimum within this huge country. Teams will expect the longest flight, depending on their base, to be around three hours.

Kazan Arena – 45379 capacity, 512 miles from Moscow; Samara (Cosmos) Arena 44,918, 661 miles; Mordovia Arena, 44,442, 377 miles; Luzhniki Stadium, 81,000, 0 miles; Otkrytive Arena, 45,360, 0 miles; St Petersburg Stadium, 68,134, 448 miles; Kaliniingrad Stadium (an enclave of Russia), 35,212, 778 miles;

Nizhny Novgorod Stadium 44,899, 264 miles; Volvograd Arena, 45,568, 606 miles; Rostov Arena (Rostov on Don), 45,000, 644 miles; Fisht Olympic Stadium, (Sochi), 47659, 1007 miles; Yekaterinburg Central Stadium; 35696, 1151 miles.

Group Stages

There were four pots, each of eight teams. Pot One contained the seven highest ranked teams plus the hosts. Pot two the next eight highest ranked and so on. These pots were then used to make eight groups, with one team from each pot. There could be one team only from each confederation (Africa, South America etc) except for Europe, which could have a maximum of two teams. Russia were pre-drawn into group A.

Group A

Russia, Uruguay, Egypt, Saudi Arabia

14/6 Russia v Saudi Arabia *Luzhniki Stadium, Moscow*

15/6 Egypt v Uruguay *Central Stadium, Yekaterinburg*

19/6 Russian v Egypt *Krestovsky Stadium, St Petersburg*

20/6 Uruguay v Saudi Arabia *Rostov Arena, Rostov*

25/6 Uruguay v Russia *Cosmos Arena, Samara*

Saudi Arabia v Egypt *Volvograd Arena, Volvograd*

Group B

Portugal, Spain, Iran, Morocco

15/6 Morocco v Iran *Krestovsky Stadium, St Petersburg*

Portugal v Spain *Fisht Olympic Stadium, Sochi*

20/6 Portugal v Morocco *Luzhniki Stadium, Moscow*

Iran v Spain *Kazan Arena, Kazan*

25/6 Iran v Portugal *Mordovia Arena, Saransk*

Spain v Morocco *Kalingrad Stadium, Kalingrad*

Group C

France, Peru, Denmark, Australia

16/6 Spain v Australia *Kazan Arena, Kazan*

Peru v Denmark *Mordovia Arena, Saransk*

21/6 Spain v Peru *Central Stadium, Yekaterinburg*

Denmark v Australia *Cosmos Arena, Samara*

26/6 Denmark v Spain *Luzhniki Stadium, Moscow*

Australia v Peru *Fisht Olympic Stadium, Sochi*

Group D

Argentina, Croatia, Iceland, Nigeria

16/6 Argentina v Iceland *Otkrytiye Arena*

Croatia v Nigeria *Kalingrad Stadium, Kalingrad*

21/6 Argentina v Croatia *Nizhny Novgorod Stadium, Nizhny Novgorod*

22/6 Nigeria v Iceland *Volvograd Arena, Volvograd*

26/6 Nigeria v Argentina *Krestovsky Stadium, St Petersburg*

Iceland v Croatia *Rostov Arena, Rostov*

Group E

Brazil, Switzerland, Costa Rica, Serbia

17/6 Costa Rica v Serbia *Cosmos Arena, Samara*

Brazil v Switzerland *Rostov Arena, Rostov*

22/6 Brazil v Costa Rica *Krestovsky Stadium, St Petersburg*

Serbia v Switzerland *Kalingrad Stadium, Kalingrad*

27/6 Serbia v Brazil *Otkrytiye Arena, Moscow*

Switzerland v Costa Rica *Nizhny Novgorod Stadium, Nizhny Novgorod*

Group F

Germany, Mexico, Sweden, Korea

17/6 Germany v Mexico *Luzhniki Stadium, Moscow*

18/6 Sweden v Korea *Nizhny Novgorod Stadium, Nizhny Novgorod*

23/6 Germany v Sweden *Fisht Olympic Stadium, Sochi*

Korea v Mexico *Rostov Arena, Rostov*

27/6 Korea v Germany *Kazan Arena, Kazan*

Mexico v Sweden *Central Stadium, Yekaterinburg*

Group G

Belgium, England, Tunisia, Panama

18/6 Belgium v Panama *Fisht Olympic Stadium, Sochi*

Tunisia v England *Volgograd Arena, Volgograd*

23/6 Belgium v Tunisia *Otkrytiye Arena, Moscow*

24/6 England v Panama *Nizhny Novgorod Stadium, Nizhny Novgorod*

28/6 England v Belgium *Kalingrad Stadium, Kalingrad*

Panama v Tunisia *Morodovia Arena, Saransk*

Group H

Poland, Colombia, Senegal, Japan

19/6 Poland v Senegal *Otkrytiye Arena, Moscow*

Colombia v Japan *Morodovia Arena, Saransk*

24/6 Japan v Senegal *Central Stadium, Yekaterinburg*

Poland v Colombia *Kazan Arena, Kazan*

28/6 Japan v Poland *Volgograd Arena, Volgograd*

Senegal v Colombia *Cosmos Arena, Samara*

Criteria for Qualification

The top two in each group qualify for the last sixteen. Positions are decided by:

- Points
- Goal difference
- Goals scored

Then, for the anoraks, if needed:

- Points obtained in matches between teams who are level
- Goal difference between these teams
- Goals scored between these teams
- Fair play (yellow card = -1, two yellows/red = -3, straight red -4, yellow then straight red -5)
- Lots

Knockout Stages

All matches have 90 minutes, then extra time if needed, finally penalties if needed.

Last 16

30/6 *Sochi*, Match 49 Winner A v Runner up B

30/6 *Kazan*, Match 50 Winner C v Runner up D

2/7 *Samara*, Match 53 Winner E v Runner up F

2/7 *Rostov*, Match 54 Winner G v Runner Up H

1/7 *Moscow* (L), Match 51 Winner B v Runner up A

1/7 *Nizhny*, Match 52 Winner D v Runner up C

3/7 *St Petersburg*, Match 55 Winner F v Runner up E

3/7 *Moscow (O),* Match 56 Winner H v Runner up G

Quarter Finals

6/7 *Nizhny*, Match 57 Winner 49 v Winner 50

6/7 *Kazan*, Match 58 Winner 53 v Winner 54

7/7 *Sochi*, Match 59 Winner 51 v Winner 52

7/7 *Samara*, Match 60 Winner 55 v Winner 56

Semi Finals

10/7 *St. Petersburg,* Winner 57 v Winner 58

11/7 *Moscow* (L), Winner 59 v Winner 60

Third Place Play Off

14/7 *St Petersburg*, Losing semi-finalists

Final

15/7 *Moscow* (L) Winning semi finalists

Europe

Russia

World Cup Pedigree:

1994 – Group Stages, third of four

2002 – Group Stages, third of four

2014 – Group Stages, third of four

Star Man: Aleksander Kokorin.

Alexander Kokorin – could he swing it for the hosts?

Kokorin is on the crest of a wave since former Man. City boss Roberto Mancini became coach at Zenit St Petersburg. In 2014, the player was Russia's surprising star man, being just 23 at the time. But his form wavered and he was left out of the Confederations Cup competition earlier in 2017. Now, since his form burst forwards domestically, he is very much back in the fold.

His preferred position is centre forward but he can play on the wing. Kokorin is a clinical finisher who also possesses an eye for an assist.

If Russia are to get to the latter stages, they will need their striker to be at his best.

Who Might We Know?

'Not many', is the answer here. In all likelihood, the entire squad will be Russia based, although some of the team have Brazilian heritage.

On top of Kokorin, possibly Aleksandr Golovin might be best known, but largely for drawing comparisons with a more well-known Russian (he played in

England, although not particularly successfully, one match versus Liverpool apart) Andrey Arshavin, the former Arsenal player.

Manager: Stanislav Cherchesov

Prospects:

This is Russia, home nation of a World. Many will look to read between the lines and feel that the nation might out perform their ranking and expectations. Having said that, being at home in a county where nationalistic passions can run riot, there is every chance that they will have the motivation to better than form suggests.

At number 65 in the charts, they are the lowest ranked nation in the tournament and there is not a lot to suggest that the ranking is misleading.

But there will be intense pressure to at least reach the knock out stages, and then anything can happen. The Russian public (and their political leaders) are notoriously unforgiving towards failure and although three defeats are on the cards, don't be too surprised to see them squeeze through.

Road to the Finals:

As the host nation, Russia did not need to qualify for the tournament.

Player from the Past: Oleg Salenko, there's a name to recall. The only player to score five in a single match at a World Cup finals.

When the Soviet Union broke up in the early 1990s, Salenko could have played for either Russia or Ukraine. But as the latter had not qualified for the 1994 world cup, he made the decision to join the newly formed Russian team.

And what a fine decision it turned out to be. By the time of the final group game, Russia were effectively out of the running to reach the next stage, and centre forward Salenko had scored just one, the opener in a three one defeat against Sweden.

But then the final match, versus the Cameroon (who had pushed England close in the quarter final of the previous World Cup), and Oleg Salenko found his moments (several of them) of glory.

His first goal saw him place a loose ball firmly home; the second, a stretched finish when put through one on one with the Cameroon keeper. His hat trick came with a low penalty to his right, which sent the goalie the wrong way and number four saw him on the end of a fine team move, driving the ball home from fifteen yards. His final goal, in both the match and the tournament, saw him once again put through one on one with the keeper, this time he lifted it over the on-rushing player into the far corner.

The unlikely hero had won a share of the Golden Boot at the USA World Cup.

After retiring, he became briefly manager of a beach football team before returning to his first international side, the Ukraine (he was capped once, in 1992), where he works for their football federation.

Germany

World Cup Pedigree:

Good enough to win at Crufts, and the current team suggests that this could be another World Cup of German domination.

The Germans know how progress through a tournament. Only once have they failed to reach at least the last eight.

Only twice have they failed to appear – they did not enter the first competition in 1930 and were banned from the 1950 tournament owing to some political wrong doing during the previous decade, more commonly defined as starting World War II.

From the end of that conflict until the collapse of the Berlin Wall, they played as West Germany, but we have included their records of this time.

1934 – Third

1938 – First round, lost to Switzerland

1954 – Winners

1958 – Fourth

1962 – Quarter finals

1966 – Runners up

1970 - Third

1974 – Winners

1978 – Second group qualifying stage (last eight, came third of four in their group)

1982 – Runners up

1986 – Runners up

1990 – Winners

1994 – Quarter finals

1998 – Quarter finals

2002 – Runners up

2006 – Third place

2010 – Third place

2014 – Winners

Star Man – Mesut Ozil

Really, it is take your pick from a whole range of players, but Ozil is the man who can destroy an opponent with his insightful passing.

Among the overwhelming majority of Arsenal fans, he is deeply loved and his class on the pitch oozes like liquid gold from a smelting machine. But as an international he moves up to a different class.

Perhaps because he is offered some protection by referees from the sort of nudging and knocking that is accepted in the Premier League, he dominates matches and has been named the German player of the year more times than not during his international career.

Watching him destroy poor Gareth Barry in the 2010 World Cup should be a video with an X rating. And now, aged 29, he is at the peak of his abilities. Frightening (unless, dear reader, you are a supporter of Germany).

Who Might We Know?

There will be no unknown names in the squad, and many of those players likely to be picked ply their trade in the Premier league.

On top of Ozil, expect to see his team mate Shkodran Mustafi, the Manchester City duo Leroy Sane and Ilkay Gundogan, plus Chelsea's Antonio Rudiger and Liverpool' Emre Can.

Add to these the likes of Toni Krus, Thomas Mueller and the world's best keeper (possibly), Manuel Neuer and we can see why they are pre-tournament favourites.

Manager – Joachim Lowe

Prospects

It is hard to see the Germans not progressing to at least the semifinals, and there are not too many who would be against them lifting the trophy at the end. They are the number one ranked team on the planet.

The German production line of success could well mean the sky's the limit once again.

However, while it is surely unimaginable that they will not get through the group stages, their prospects of becoming World Champions yet again will not be far short of an even bet.

Nobody is going to want to draw the Germans, but there are teams capable of beating them in a one off, and possible opponents who might cause a problem or two include Brazil and France, and England did manage a draw. Their second round opponents are unlikely to present any concerns but England or Belgium might offer a challenge in the quarter finals

In the old days, of course, qualification as reigning champions would have been automatic, but the team will benefit from having had to take part in a qualifying campaign, with recent, serious matches having been played.

In the past, with two years between major competitions in Europe, too many friendlies meant sides were less tournament ready. This might explain why the cup has failed to be retained since Brazil in 1962, and the only other team to do so was Italy back in the early, pre-war competitions.

Road to the Finals:

Having just made the case for some advantage for Germany in having to play through a qualification group, of course that group was extremely straight forward.

Played ten, won ten, scoring an average of more than four goals per game. Their opponents were Northern Ireland, the Czech Republic, Norway plus the mighty Azerbaijan and San Marino.

Player from the Past: Harald Schumacher

Who can forget THAT challenge back in 1982. A magnificent ball from the maestro Michel Platini sets away the young forward Patrick Battiston; one on one with the onrushing keeper, he volleys just wide.

But that keeper is Harald Schumacher, tight shorted and curly haired, he leaps six yards from the striker and lands, many moments after the ball has passed him, full into the face and body of the striker.

The referee, Dutchman Charles Corver, for a reason nobody (including he) will probably ever know, awards a goal kick and takes no further action, and with players of both teams surrounding the prone Frenchman, waves the game on.

Only after intervention from those players, does he call for assistance for the unconscious striker.

Following the event, Schumacher took a single-minded approach, despite Battiston losing two teeth, needing oxygen on the pitch and incurring three cracked ribs. He said that he had done nothing wrong, and only later did he apologise for the consequences of his actions.

It is a shame for Schumacher that this one event is that with which he is forever associated. He was a fine keeper, the German number one for their campaigns in the 1980s.

However, he did find controversy hard to avoid. His publication of an autobiography in which he claimed substance abuse from many of his team mates saw him isolated in German football, and he retains the unusual and unwelcome accolade of being sacked during half time as a coach.

Portugal

World Cup Pedigree

Not until the great Eusebio came onto the scene did football mad Portugal make it to a World Cup finals. What a difference he made, being top scorer with nine goals in their inaugural competition, the 1966 finals in England, where the hosts and eventual winners knocked them out in the semi finals. They are the current European Champions.

1966 – Third

1986 – Group stages – fourth of four

2002 – Group stages – third of four

2006 – Fourth

2010 – Last sixteen

2014 – Group stages – third of four

Star Man: Pepe

OK, we could play safe and go for Ronaldo, but the great player will be 33 by the time of the finals and whether that pace and fear factor will still be there with non-stop games remains to be seen.

Eusebio – One of the all-time greats

Portugal, unless their star man defies the years in truly astonishing fashion (and he might), will need a tough, uncompromising defensive presence.

Cue Pepe. After ten years with Real Madrid, it seemed as though the hard man might be winding down, but his performances alongside much weaker team mates at Besiktas demonstrate that the player, admittedly in his mid-thirties, is playing the best football of his considerable career.

Age is less of problem for a defender, particularly one such as Pepe where reading of the game and uncompromising interventions mark his play, and he could just be the man if Portugal are to have any chance of living up to their rather ridiculously high world ranking.

Who Might We Know?

Of course, Ronaldo and Pepe are two of their biggest names, but a number of the likely squad parade their talents on these islands.

Nelson Oliveira is performing well for Norwich and Bruno Alves continues to ply his trade, now for Rangers. Although, as another player in his mid-thirties, whether he makes the cut remains to be seen.

Several of Portugal's finest play in the Premier league, including Bernardo Silva for Manchester City. Adrien Silva is on Leicester City's books, Jose Fonte plays for West Ham, Cedric Soares for Southampton and Renato Sanches is impressing people on loan with Swansea City.

Manager: Fernando Santos

Road to the Finals

One of the tougher European groups saw the Euro 2016 champions drawn in the same pool as Hungary and Switzerland.

Portugal just about topped the group, winning every match after an initial defeat away to the Swiss. Evidence that his skills are fading... Ronaldo scored a mere fifteen times during qualification.

Prospects:

Ranked three in the World, the aging Portuguese sit alongside Poland and Russia as the teams from Pot One most sides would like to draw.

So much of their success has been based on a tough back line and the genius of Ronaldo, but anno dominia is catching up and prospects look average at best.

Realistically, they should progress through the group stages, but whether the Seleccaos can get much further is seriously open to question.

Last sixteen would be acceptable, given their squad, last eight would represent a good campaign.

But then again, they do have Ronaldo...

Player from the Past – Eusebio

The stocky striker is, along with Ronaldo, one of the two greatest Portuguese players in world football history. Playing at a time when Pele was also at his peak, his stronger frame protected him from some of the rough treatment the World's greatest ever player suffered from.

It was not just leading Portugal to third place in the 1966 World Cup that marked him out as a superstar.

Nor his astonishing scoring record of forty-one goals in just sixty-four internationals. He led the legendary Benfica team of the 1960s, playing for fourteen years in the side. Benfica won the European Cup in both 1961 (without their young star) and 62, before coming in as runners up in 1963, '65 and '68.

The skills of the legendary 'Black Panther' were astonishing. His strength and low centre of gravity made him hard to dispossess and he had a lethal eye for goal. He played for his club more than six hundred times, and averaged more than a goal a game.

Belgium

World Cup Pedigree

With a population of just eleven and a third million, alongside a passion for chocolate and waffles, the Belgians really punch above their weight. They have no particularly major European forces among their club sides (apologies to fans of FC Bruges and so forth) but they are experiencing a golden generation at the moment...even if nearly every player is based abroad.

Is football currently Belgium's best export? And what about the chocolate? And the EU? And the sprouts? Belgium's got the lot.

1930 – First round

1934 – First round

1938 – First round

1954 – Group stage fourth of four

1970 – Group stage third of four

1982 – Second Group stage, third of three

1986 – Fourth

1990 – Last sixteen

1994 – Last sixteen

1998 – Group stage third of four (but unbeaten!!)

2002 – Last sixteen

2014 – Quarter finals

Star Man: Romalu Lukaku

The Manchester United forward is tailor made for a side that likes to play football. And that means any team under Roberto Martinez.

With quality midfielders to offer a quality supply he could well take the Golden Boot and that might be enough to send the Trophy to Brussels.

Who Might We know?

The Belgian squad reads like a who's who of Premier league all-stars. Alderweireld, Dembele and Vertonghen (Spurs) are joined by Batshuayi, Courtois and Eden Hazard from Chelsea. De Bruyne and Kompany from the blue half of Manchester will combine with Fellaini and Lukaku from the red side. Add to that Steven Defour (Burnley), Simon Mignolet and Divock Origi (Liverpool) Nacer Chadli (West Brom), Kevin Mirallas (Everton) Christian Benteke (Palace) and Christian Kabasele (Watford). Don't forget Celtic's Dedryck Boyata… it is clear who the Brits might support when England bite the turf.

Manager: Roberto Martinez

Road to the Finals

With an incredible forty goals scored in qualification, admittedly against some weak sides (they scored twenty-three in three matches against Gibraltar and Estonia), there is no doubting the effectiveness of the Red Devils' attack. Just a disappointing home draw with Greece the only grass stain on the knees.

Prospects

They should be one of the favourites for the tournament. Certainly, if the strongest eleven come together, they will be capable of beating anybody.

There are two main risks which could hit at any time during the knock out stages. Firstly, as brilliant as they are going forward, will Martinez be prepared to shut up shop against say, a Brazil, Germany (their probable quarter final opponents come from these two) or Argentina or will the free-flowing football lead to gaps in midfield and, subsequently, defeat?

Secondly, while that top eleven is really strong, a couple of injuries and latter stage suspensions could expose the lack of depth the Belgians possess.

They would be very popular winners of the tournament, but many pundits feel that the competition experience of Germany or France, Brazil or Argentina might just prevail.

Player from the Past: Raymond Braine

This clever striker scored at an unbelievable rate in his career, which ran from the 1925 until it was curtailed by the outbreak of World War II. He scored 26 times for Belgium, but it was his club performances that really impressed.

He scored 141 goals in 143 matches with Beerschot VAC before becoming the first Belgian professional and joining Sparta Prague, where he netted 120 times in just 106 games. He returned to Beerschot in 1936, having turned down an offer of Czech citizenship, and continued to play on during the conflict, but, of course, international football pretty much ceased during the war years in Europe.

Poland

World Cup Pedigree

1938 – First round (lost to Brazil 6-5…more on this match later)

1974 – Third

1978 – Second group stage, third of four

1982 – Third

1986 – Last sixteen

2002 – Group stage, fourth of four

2006 – Group stage, third of four

Star Player – Robert Lewandowski

Who Might We know?

Only a couple of Premier League players, plus a pair from the championship. Lukasz Fabianski is the Swansea 'keeper, and Grzegorz Krychowiak plays for West Brom. Pawel Wszolek turns out for QPR and Kamil Grosicki is on the books of Hull City.

Manager: Adam Nawalka. Quite a journey for the Pole; after an injury wrecked his career, he emigrated to the US and felled trees before returning home and selling Trabant cars. He works with higher quality products these days.

Road to the Finals

A relatively comfortable qualification. The 4-0 defeat away to Denmark happened when the Poles had already qualified, and the Danes are a more than decent outfit these days.

The only real blip was a draw away to lowly Kazakhstan in the opening fixture. Having said that, the team are heavily reliant on Lewandowski for their goals and (apart from a 6-1 thrashing of Armenia) did not often cruise their way to victory.

Prospects

Quite where there sixth place in the world ranking comes from, nobody is really sure. They were the team most Pot two teams wanted to secure. Last sixteen would seem a fair prediction.

However, it would surprise few if they were the only top seed to fail to progress beyond the group stage.

They might be from the top pot, but Poland are unlikely to win any medals.

Player from the Past – Ernst Wilimowski

The Polish German international represented both sides, and was considered one of the greatest goalscorers of all time.

He hit his peak during the war years, and scored thirteen goals in eight games during this spell, although the legitimacy of those matches is naturally called into question.

Some reports claim a career record of 1175 goals, although many of these were in friendly and matches designed to boost the public's morale.

France

World Cup Pedigree

Regular qualifiers but only occasional performers when it comes to finals. Indeed, the first tournaments in which they took part saw a very early exit as par for the course, but things have picked up since the 1980s.

1930 - Group stage, third of four

1934 - First round

1938 - Quarter final

1954 - Group stage, third of four

1958 - Third

1966 - Group stage, fourth of four

1978 – Group stage, third of four

1982 – Fourth

1986 – Third

1998 – Winners

2002 – Group stage, fourth of four

2006 – Runners up

2010 – Group stage, fourth of four

2014 – Quarter finals

Star Player: N'Golo Kante

There is a lot of flair in the French team, and somebody will need to tie that creativeness together, giving support to what may be at times an exposed defence.

That man is the Duracell battery himself, N'Golo Kante. His work rate, allied to more skill than he is often given credit for, could turn the French into very serious challengers.

Who Might We know?

Many of the French squad, including the likes of Griezmann, will be well known on British soil, with several players from the Premier league likely to be involved.

THAT tackle from Schumacher. See where the ball is.

As well as Kante, Bakayoko also plays for Chelsea, whilst defender Laurent Koscielny and strikers Olivier Giroud and Alexandre Lacazette represent Arsenal. Hugo Lloris and Moussa Sissoko are from the other side of North London and Anthony Martial and Paul Pogba represent the red side of Manchester, with Eliaquim Mangala and Benjamin Mendy from the blue. Yohan Cabaye is at the heart of Crystal Palace's midfield, and Kurt Zouma is currently representing Stoke.

Manager: Didier Deschamps

Road to the Finals

One of the tougher groups in European qualification was navigated relatively easily by France. Regular finals makers Sweden and Bulgaria joined minnows Luxembourg and Belarus alongside giants the Netherlands to provide opposition for the French.

Les Bleus qualified with twenty-three points, the third lowest, but lost only once on the campaign (away to Sweden). However, 0-0 draws against the two weakest teams in the group indicates the inconsistency of the French national side.

Prospects

Very good, potentially, allied to an equally fair risk of disappointment. The squad has reasonable depth and the first eleven are a match for anyone in the world.

Getting the best out of individual parts might be the biggest challenge for Deschamps. The French teams have often imploded unexpectedly (see results against Belarus and Luxembourg in qualification for recent evidence), and there are a number of strong characters in this team. If they stay on track, then they have a good chance of coming out as winners, but if opponents can get in their heads, who knows what will happen?

Player from the Past – Michel Platini

Le Roi graced the fields of football with a style and panache that was both astonishing and typically French. Cigarette in hand, he hardly espoused the virtues of looking after his body, but such was the talent in his feet that he was widely regarded as the greatest player in the world during his early eighties' heyday.

He led France to the European Championships and, in the same season won both the league title in Italy with Juventus, a European title and the Ballon d'Or.

But it was after his playing career ended that his story took a bizarre turn. He became the football supremo at Uefa, leading the administrative body for nine years, and was widely expected to take over from the disgraced Sepp Blatter as President of FIFA.

But when the proverbial shit hits the fan, those standing nearby are likely to gain an unpleasant smell. Platini was unable to clear his name after being accused of breaching FIFA ethics, and resigned his role.

Unlike nearly all others at the top of the game's administration, he was a man who had football at his heart AND he understood the sport as only a great purveyor of his art could.

He understood coaches. he understood managers and he 'got' players. He possessed (another rarity) a great sense of humour but allied to that was a determination to move Uefa forwards.

He had masterminded one of the best of all World Cups, the 1998 tournament hosted and won by France, and innovated the changes needed to ensure football's primacy in world sport.

He was the man behind the Financial Fair Play scheme, indeed there may well be a link between enemies he made then and his ultimate downfall.

Now those ideas have bitten the dust, and the game risks becoming the plaything of the mega-rich, to the detriment of competition and clubs outside of the financially elite.

The once supreme footballer has missed the chance of becoming a revolutionary administrator at a time the game needs such a figurehead more than ever.

Spain

World Cup Pedigree

A team with such a strong heritage, especially in recent years, to be outside the top pot is surprising, but every team that escaped Spain, even those that were in Pot 1, will be breathing a sigh of relief.

1934 – Quarter finals

1950 – Fourth

1962 – Group stage, fourth of four

1966 – Group stage, third of four

1978 – Group stage, third of four

1982 – Second group stage, third of three

1986 – Quarter finals

1990 – Last sixteen

1994 – Quarter finals

1998 – Group stage, third of four

2002 – Quarter finals

2006 – Last sixteen

2010 – Winners

2014 – Group stage, third of four

Star Player: David De Gea

It is not often that a goalkeeper is identified as possibly the best player in the team, but the Spaniard is now vying with Manuel Neuer as the best in the world.

The player has publicly expressed his happiness playing for Manchester United, despite on-going pressure to get him back to Spain with Real Madrid. That probably means he will soon be on his way.

However, he continues to gain points for his team in many matches.

The answer to Spain's prayers?

If Spain are to regain some hint of their 2008-13 supremacy, they will need him to be at the top of his game in Russia. At 27, he is approaching the peak years for goalkeepers, and that augurs well for the former champions.

Who Might We know?

There is a strong contingent from Spain in the Premier League, all from top six clubs. Of course, with Spain being home to two of the world's biggest clubs, Barcelona and Real Madrid, many of their home-based players will also be very familiar to British fans.

Juan Mata, David De Gea and Ander Herrera all play for Manchester United, and Chelsea provide Alvaro Morata, Cesar Azpilicueta and Pedro. Nacho Monreal is a reliable defender for Arsenal, Hector Bellerin is a fine attacking full back and David Silva continues to be a leading light for Manchester City.

Manager: Julien Lopetegui

Road to the Finals

Nine wins and a draw (away to Italy), with thirty six goals scored and a miserly three conceded give strength to Spain's claims to be re-emerging as one of the most talented teams in the world.

But, when we look at their qualification from Group G, and see Albania in third place, the truth becomes a little clearer. Still, Spain didn't ask for their opponents. They also had a serious challenger in the likes of Italy, although the former multiple winners did not ultimately qualify this time round.

Prospects

Middling. The great players from five to ten years ago are well past their prime, or retired altogether, and their short, rapid passing game has moved, to some extent, out of fashion.

For all that, nobody will want to play them. They have a number of very good players, and some promising youngsters coming through. How many make the squad we will have to see but Ruben Garcia, Suso and Daniel Carvajal all might make their mark in Russia.

At the same time, the point at which they meet a Germany, Brazil or suchlike suggests the time when they will probably meet their match.

Player from the Past   Raul

The great goal scorer just missed out on Spain's glory years, but his performances as a player and a role model have made him a legend in his own country.

Famously never sent off, the striker hit the professional game running, scoring sixteen times in just seven games with Real Madrid C.

Rapidly promoted to the main side he became, briefly, the youngest ever player to represent the Spanish giants. He would go on to score 323 goals for them over a long career.

He also started and ended his Real career at the same ground, La Romareda, home of Real Zaragoza.

In his thirties he would have a successful couple of seasons with Schalke, before moving to short spells in the Middle East and the US.

Always a private man, he dedicated every goal to his wife, kissing his wedding ring to honour her.

Switzerland

World Cup Pedigree

1934 – Quarter finals

1938 – Quarter finals

1950 – Group stage, third of four

1954 – Quarter finals

1962 – Group stage, fourth of four

1966 – Group stage, fourth of four

1994 – Last sixteen

2006 – Last sixteen

2010 – Group stage, third of four

2014 – Last sixteen

Star Player – Xherdan Shaqiri

The striker is developing a kind of cult status at Stoke, and has already scored (at the time of writing) twenty times for his country.

His hat-trick against Honduras at the 2014 finals was crucial in securing Switzerland's progress out of the group stages.

But once the rosy shine has gone out of Stoke fans' eyes, they will tell you that Shaqiri is not especially consistent; at his best, close to unplayable but sometimes he falls short.

The Swiss are an efficient team rather than one with stars, but somebody needs to provide a spark in any side expected to do well. Shaqiri is in the prime of his career, and could seize the opportunity to have a fine championships and get himself a move (sorry Potteries folk) back to a really big club. Then again, he may not want that. He played for Bayern Munich, Inter Milan and turned down a chance to move to Liverpool. Perhaps it was the attraction of all those chilly Tuesday nights in Shropshire that took him to Stoke.

Who Might We know?

A small number of players ply their trade in the British leagues. Granit Xhaka (Arsenal) and Xherdin Shaqiri (Stoke) are probably the best known. Edimilson Fernandes (WHU), Shani Tarashaj (Everton) and Florent Hadergjonaj (Huddersfield) are also probables for the final twenty-three.

Manager: Vladimir Petkovic

Road to the Finals

One of the luckier teams to reach the finals, they finished joint top of their group with Portugal, losing their final group match against the Portuguese which saw them slip into second place.

So, on the basis of their group games, they seem to have been solid in qualification. However, in the play offs, they drew Northern Ireland and were extremely lucky to progress.

Only one goal was scored in the entire tie, and that was one of the most astonishing decisions since Frank

Lampard buried the ball against Germany for the entire world to recognize except the officials.

A hopeful knock into the box hit defender Corry Evans on the shoulder from close range, and to the astonishment of everybody, including the Swiss players, a spot kick was awarded.

Corry's better-known brother Johnny almost pulled it back in the return leg, but his header in injury time was cleared off the line.

So, while the Swiss deserve to be in Russia on the back of their group game results, they are extremely fortunate to be getting on the plane next summer.

Prospects

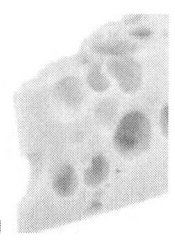

Not too many holes in the Swiss defence

The Swiss are tough to beat, and play well as a team. For a side ranked in the top twelve in the world, it is surprising that they possess no really world class players, but that is not always a disadvantage, at least in the early stages.

They must have a decent chance of progressing to the knock out stages, and once there anything could happen.

While it is hard imagining them beating the really top sides, it is not impossible by any means.

Maybe they will spend a lot of time working on their penalty taking. They could be a top tip to be involved in a short out or two. As you can see, rather in fitting with the nation, I am sitting on the fence here.

Player from the Past: Max Abegglen

Max Abegglen is celebrated in the name of Swiss side Neuchatel Xamax, a rare accolade indeed. Abegglen's nickname was Xam. (Xam-Max, geddiit?) Possibly the greatest Swiss footballer of all time, he missed out on ever representing his country in the World Cup.

However, fifteen years in the team saw him average a goal every other game in his 68-cap career, which came to an end against a Nazi Germany team in 1937.

That scoring record stood as a high for a Swiss player until almost the turn of the current century.

However, although he did not ever get to play in the ultimate footballing tournament, he was instrumental in helping the Swiss to gain a silver medal in the Olympics. He also played alongside two brothers in the National team.

Croatia

World Cup Pedigree

Of course, prior to gaining independence in 1991, Croatia was a part of the former Yugoslavia. They did not gain entry to Fifa until 1993, which meant that they were too late for the US finals the following year. Therefore, their history in the competition is limited.

1998 – Third

2002 – Group stage, third of four

2006– Group stage, third of four

2014– Group stage, third of four

Star Player : Luka Modric

At 32, the tricky midfielder has lost none of his guile and remains a key pin in the Real Madrid midfield. He has been picked in the World XI for three consecutive seasons up to the 2017/18 campaigns, and has been player of the year in his home country five times. He has over a hundred caps as well as three Champions' League winners' medals.

Is there a strategy for success available to the chequer-board shirts?

A deep lying playmaker, with brilliant vision, Modric is also a quiet man, who likes to keep out of the limelight. He is married with two children, and will be the key if Croatia are to progress beyond the last sixteen.

Who Might We know?

A couple of players appear in the Premiership. Dejan Lovren didn't have the greatest of starts to the 2017 season with Liverpool, and Nikola Vlasic turns out for Everton.

In addition, Mario Mandzukic plays for Juventus and striker Nikola Kalinic represents AC Milan.

Manager: Zlatko Dalic

Road to the Finals

Croatia defeated Greece in the play offs, winning 4-1 at home before securing a 0-0 in the away leg.

They had an interesting group, which although it contained no superstar teams, nevertheless had four sides all capable of getting through. Iceland, in their current vein of never before experienced form, topped the group but Croatia ensured that the Ukraine and Turkey finished below them.

Even Finland were not a pushover team, and only Kosovo had no chance of qualification.

Given the quality of the opposition, that they conceded only four goals in ten matches, and lost 1-0 to Turkey and Iceland (both away) indicates that they will be tough to beat in Russia.

Prospects

Croatia will be tough opponents for anybody. They are strong defensively and have been well organized, although their current coach was appointed only at the very end of the qualification campaign.

Equally, it does not look as though they will score many. Some of the better-known players in the squad are getting on a bit, and how they will cope in the latter stages, when matches have hit hard and regularly is hard to tell.

They should get through the group round, and might even succeed through a couple of rounds in the latter stages, but do not have the class to progress beyond that. Then again, teams do win competitions on the back of 1-0s and penalty shoot outs.

Player from the Past: Davor Suker

The brilliant striker, top scorer at the 1998 World Cup was voted Croatia's best player on no less than six occasions.

Suker was and is a passionate patriot, for whom the civil war must have been deeply influential. He is a controversial figure, accused of holding severe right-wing views. He was banned for ten matches by Fifa when he shouted an infamous Ustase (the organization of hard-line Croatian fighters) slogan 'Za som – spremni!' (For home – ready!) Presumably, for Fifa at that time, corruption was fine while political beliefs were not.

Like Michel Platini, following his playing career he moved into football politics, but once again controversy followed him.

Publicizing himself in the third person as a brand – 'Davor Suker is a brand' he once said - he was criticized as president of the Croatian football federation for being a puppet to his vice president.

Nevertheless, more former players are needed at the top of the world footballing organizations if the sport is properly to be represented. Suker may still come close to achieving as much off the pitch as he did on it.

Denmark

World Cup Pedigree

So, we move into those European qualifiers who were seeded in Pot 3, based on their Fifa rankings.

Denmark are down at 21, in Premier league terms, a Championship side. If that is their level, we reckon that they are definitely due for promotion. It took the Danes until 1986 to qualify for the first time, but their record has improved since then.

1986 – Last sixteen

1998 – Quarter finals

2002 – Last sixteen

2010 – Group stage, third of four

Star Player: Christian Eriksen

Denmark's star man.

At the time of writing (late Autumn, 2017), the skillfulTottenham midfielder was in the form of his life.

Always talented, he had the reputation among Spurs followers of never quite delivering when the chips were down, but his performances are earning terrific plaudits and his hat-trick away to the Republic of Ireland in the qualifiers cemented his position as a world class player.

He is also a dead ball specialist and that means there is always a hope of a goal, even against the toughest opposition.

Who Might We know?

There are few players plying their trade in the top divisions in England.

Kasper Schmeichel plays for Leicester, Erikson for Spurs and Huddersfield offer Jonas Lossi and Mathias Jorgensen. Pierre-Emile Hojbjerg (Southampton) and Andreas Christensen (Chelsea) complete the Premier league line up. From the championship, three Brentford players might get call ups – Henrik Dalsgard, Andreas Bjelland and Lasse Vibe, whilst Middlesbrough's Martin Braithwaite and Jonas Knudsen from Ipswich also could feature.

Manager: Age Hareide

Road to the Finals

Denmark reached the play offs from a moderate group which was topped by Poland. They scored well and defended effectively, losing just twice (surprisingly home to Montenegro, less strangely away to Poland).

Prospects

Denmark have a good record at World Cups when they qualify, usually progressing from the group stages.

With an in form Eriksen and the rub of the green, they could get out of their group, and have the talent to worry sides, but it is hard to see them getting much further than the knock out first round, if that.

Player from the Past – Peter Schmeichel

Very few footballers have the honour of a part of the game becoming named after them; the Cruyff turn associated with the Dutch superstar is one such example, while Diego Maradona probably finds the Hand of God allusion less appealing.

To 'Schmeichel' means to approach an oncoming striker and dive in a star shape to prevent the one on one scoring opportunity.

How brilliantly the former Manchester United and Denmark keeper did this, gaining him the coveted title as the best goalie in the world for a spell, winning the award in both 1992 and 1993.

He also won a poll of 200000 supporters who voted him the best goalkeeper of all time, beating even the legendary Gordon Banks and Lev Yashin.

Since retirement he has enjoyed the various diverse activities of owning his own football club, being a pundit, working in the media (including taking part in several quiz shows) and hosting a quiz show of his own.

He was even immortalized in the popular soap opera, Coronation Street, when a character named his dog, Schmeichel.

Iceland

World Cup Pedigree...first time qualifiers

Iceland will be the smallest ever nation to play in a World Cup finals. Their population is around just 350000 people; winning the competition would be like Leicester City triumphing against hugely bigger teams...and that would never happen, would it?

Iceland's most effective player?

Star Player: Gylfi Siggurdson

The Everton midfielder had a tough start to the season, but it is unlikely to impact on his performances at this, the biggest event ever in Iceland's footballing history.

Beating England at Euro 2016 was amazing enough, but the chance of mixing it with the world's best, maybe for the only chance in a life time, will be an incredible motivator for all of the team.

Sigurdsson is their biggest name these days, and his brilliance with a dead ball will always give them a chance.

Who Might We know?

Although it is a golden generation for Iceland, they remain a team with few stars. A small number play in Britain including, in addition to Sigurdsson, Johann Berg Gudmundsson from Burnley. Kari Arnason plays for Aberdeen in the Scottish Premier, and Aron Gunnarsson (Cardiff), Jon Dadi Bodvarsson (Reading), Birkir Bjarnason (Aston Villa) and Horour Bjorgvin Magnusson (Bristol City) all play in the English Championship.

Manager: The ever smiling Heimir Hallgrimsson

Road to the Finals

Iceland topped their group, itself a remarkable achievement made more so by the fact that, under normal circumstances, Croatia, Ukraine, Turkey and Finland would all consider them easy meat.

But the Icelandic team kept on running and trundled its way to 22 points, losing only twice during the campaign.

Prospects

Backed by their Viking supporters, and being every neutral's favourite side, and the number two team for all other fans the Icelanders will come into the tournament with a gale of support behind them.

And that might be enough to sweep them into the knock out stages. They probably don't have enough to beat the best, but we can be sure that they will give it a try.

In fact, the only people who might not want them to do that well are the match commentators who, when identifying players, will need to get all of their 'sons' in the right order.

Player from the Past – Eidur Smari Gudjohnsen

The blond forward certainly got around. Playing professionally until his late thirties, he represented no fewer than sixteen clubs, occasionally on loan, scoring over a hundred goals in five hundred appearances.

The peak of his career saw him at Chelsea, where he managed nearly one goal every three games. After six years at Stamford Bridge, he moved on to Barcelona, then Monaco.

Gudjohnsen made his international debut in the Under 17 team when he was just fourteen years old.

But perhaps his greatest international moment was unique. His father was also an international footballer, and the two were selected for the same match, against Estonia.

His 34-year-old father started the game, until he was substituted, replaced by his seventeen year old son.

In fact, the decision was political. Both were due to be selected from the outset, but the President of the Football Association of Iceland wanted the moment they started together to be on home soil.

Unfortunately, shortly after the Estonia match, Eidur sustained a serious leg injury, and did not recover until his father had retired.

However, he went on to become Iceland's all time leading scorer, and probably their greatest ever player.

Sweden

World Cup Pedigree

1934 - Quarter final

1938 – Fourth

1950 – Third

1958 – Runners up

1970 – Group stage, third of four

1974 – Second group stage, third of four

1978 – Group stage, fourth of four

1990 – Group stage, fourth of four

1994 – Third

2002 – Last sixteen

2006 – Last sixteen

Star Player: Marcus Berg

The Al Ain striker was in sparkling form during the group stages, scoring eight times. Somebody will have to replace Zlatan Ibrahimović, and that definitely won't be easy, but Berg is attracting attention from some of the bigger European clubs, and a fine finals might secure him a great move.

How the Swedes would love a player like this

This is not a golden generation time for Sweden, but they demonstrated in the play offs the ability to tackle some of the bigger teams (albeit perhaps the weakest Italian side for years); players like Berg will be vital if they are to make neighbouring Russia a party land in the summer.

Who Might We know?

Not many these days. Victor Lindelof is on Manchester United's books but most non-supporters will be unaware of that. Martin Olsson is a regular for Swansea City, who also employ Kristoffer Nordfeldt.

Mikael Lustig plays for Celtic and Pontas Jansson plays for Leeds in the Championship. If he makes the squad, Hull's Seb Larsson could present opponents with danger from set pieces.

Manager: Janne Andersson

Road to the Finals

Overcoming the Dutch was a feather in the cap of the Swedes, who also had France and Bulgaria in their group.

They scored freely in the qualifiers, and that will give them some hope in the real thing, but most impressive was their victory over Italy in the play offs.

Prospects

It is hard to see this particular group getting beyond the group stages this time round. The Swedes are well organized, and have competent players, but lack the flair to perform at the highest levels.

Mind you, that hasn't always stopped teams from winning. Think Greece and Denmark in the Euros.

Player from the Past: Erik Nilsson

Nobody achieved as much internationally for Sweden as their left back, Erik Nilsson. His career spanned the war years, and he would certainly have achieved more and won additional caps had that conflict not occurred.

From his teens, Nilsson was a one-man club, rejecting overtures from AC Milan in the process of winning five league titles and five Swedish cups.

Internationally, he was one of only two players to play in World Cups either side of the war, (the other was the Swiss, Alfred Bickel) and won both Gold and Bronze in the Olympics, and a third and fourth place in his two world cups.

A true legend.

Serbia

The lowest ranked European team to qualify for the World Cup (Russia are lower, but did not have to qualify), they are also the only team to appear in Pot 4.

World Cup Pedigree

Known as Serbia and Montenegro for the 2002 and 2006 World cups, and Yugoslavia prior to that, which included a long period where they nation was banned from competition following the Balkans' conflict. Therefore, the pedigree of Serbia is better than the list below might suggest.

2010 – Group stage, fourth of four

Star Player: Branislav Ivanovic

Although his highly successful time with Chelsea may have petered out, Ivanovic has found top form again with Zenit St Petersburg.

A stalwart in defence, he might lack a bit of pace but the underpowered Serbs will need his force of personality if they are to make any progress in the tournament.

Ivanovic is also the sort of defender who is likely to pop up with a goal or two – only John Terry scored more from the back than he while at Chelsea.

He won the Champions League, Europa League, a league cup and three Premier League titles and FA cups with the blues, and would like to see the latter days of his international career to go out with fireworks rather than damp squibs.

It is probably too much to ask of this Serbian team, however.

Who Might We know?

Nemanja Matic (Man Utd) is playing well again, and Dusan Tadic can be influential for Southampton. Lazar Markovic is on Liverpool's books, and Aleksander Mitrovic is a combative striker with Newcastle, although he loses his cool still too easily.

Manager: Slavoljub Muslin

Road to the Finals

Perhaps the easiest of all the groups, the main opposition came from Wales and the Republic of Ireland, with Austria struggling throughout.

Given this, Serbia still had to win their matches, and form would suggest that they would be beaten by the three teams named above.

Passionate, but sometimes troublesome – Serbian fans

Prospects

They have fervent support, from not the best-behaved fans in the world (this, of course, being a generalization) and it is important that any trouble does not distract the team from focusing on their best.

Even so, it is hard to imagine them getting out of the group stages. Serbia will be tough to beat, but their best players are getting on, and beaten they will eventually be.

Player from the Past: Dragan Stojković

A bit of a cheat this one, as although a Serb, he represented Yugoslavia. A fantastically talented midfielder, injury stopped him reaching his full potential for much of his career.

However, he was the star of the Yugoslav team at World Cups in 1990 and later, as captain, in 1998. He also is one of only five players to be awarded the Star of the Red Star.

He moved from the Belgrade Club to Marseilles and ended up against his former side in the final of the European Cup, but refused to take a penalty against his former cup when the match went to a shoot-out.

The current long serving Arsenal manager, Arsene Wenger, took him to Grampus Eight, in Japan, in 1994, and that was the country where he played his best ever football. Such was his cult status there that he was awarded the Order of the Rising Sun, 4th class, from the Japanese Government.

South America

Brazil

World Cup Pedigree

The only team to appear in every tournament.

1930 – Group stage, second of three

1934 – First round, second of three

1938 - Third

1950 – Runners up

1954 – Quarter final

1958 - Winners

1962 - Winners

1966 – Group stage, third of four

1970 - Winners

1974 - Fourth

1978 - Third

1982 – Second group stage, second of three

1986 – Quarter finals

1990 – Last sixteen

1994 - Winners

1998 – Runners up

2002 - Winners

2006 – Quarter finals

2010 – Quarter finals

2014 - Fourth

Star Player: Tite, the Coach

After six games the Brazilians had just nine points and had won only two games. They were sixth in the table and the very serious possibility of the unthinkable was becoming an ever-growing risk.

Then Dunga, an old school, fierce coach was replaced by Tite, a calm, seasoned professional who transformed the canary yellow team.

There is so much attacking talent in this squad that the only rival to its collective potential would be a challenge from some rather large egos.

Therefore, a coach is needed who can keep everybody in check and playing their best. Tite seems to have those skills in abundance, and this could well prove to be the most important single contribution to a strong run in Russia.

Who Might We know?

Most of the names will trip off the tongue, but those playing in the Premier league include the Manchester City trio of Ederson, Fernandinho and Jesus, the Liverpool duo of Coutinho and Firmino and Chelsea's Willian and Luiz.

Manager: Tite

Road to the Finals

As we saw above, a terrible start to the campaign threatened catastrophe for a short while, before matters were transformed by the arrival of a calm and authoritative coach. In the end, the most competitive group in the world saw Brazil out on top by an incredible ten points, as pressure began to shift onto Argentina (who made it) and Chile (who didn't).

Pele – the greatest ever player? Actually, that shouldn't need a question mark.

Prospects

If they hang together, definitely one of the favourites. The biggest threat is dissatisfaction within the squad, but risks of that do seem to be calmed for the present.

However, who would have predicted them crashing 7-1 to Germany at the last tournament? The risk that things could go bottoms up always lingers in the background.

But with such attacking talent, they will always back themselves to score more than the opposition.

If the draw works out, it would be a good bet to wager a few shillings on the last four consisting of Belgium, Germany and Brazil, with one of Argentina or France completing the set.

Player from the Past: Hilderaldo Bellini

Of course, Pele was the greatest player of all time, but there are so many attacking geniuses who have worn the yellow shirt that it is interesting to look at that other part of the game without which no team can be successful.

And perhaps the greatest Brazilian defender of all was Hilderaldo Luiz Bellini, and it won't come as too much of a surprise to learn that the player came from Italian stock.

Bellini won the World Cup in both 1958 and 1962, and also took part in the country's disappointing campaign in 1966, although by then aged 36 many of his formidable powers were in decline.

He was the first Brazilian to lift the famous Jules Rimet trophy, and did something which has become an everyday occurrence among all cup winning sides.

It was Bellini who first lifted a trophy above his head in celebration. He allegedly did so to enable photographers to get a better picture, but the gesture became associated with the euphoria of victory and has not only hung around in football, but spread to other sports and competitions.

Indeed, a statue of Bellini, trophy aloft and standing on top of the world graces the entrance to the magnificent Maracanã stadium.

Bellini was a defender of the old school, tough and unforgiving – he didn't score goals, his job was to stop them. At the same time, he possessed a touch of Latin flair when he needed it.

Argentina

World Cup Pedigree

1930 – Runners up

1934 – First round

1958 – Group stage, fourth of four

1962 – Group stage, third of four

1966 – Quarter finals

1974 – Second group stage, fourth of four

1978 - Winners

1982 – Second group stage, third of three

1986 - Winners

1990 – Runners up

1994 – Last sixteen

1998 – Quarter finals

2002 – Group stage, third of four

2006 – Quarter finals

2010 – Quarter finals

2014 – Runners up

Star Player: Lionel Messi

Having been voted as the world's best player on no fewer than five occasions, he will want to go one step further than last time and lift the trophy.

His hat trick in the last qualifying game secured a place at the finals for Argentina, and given that he will be in his mid-thirties by the time of the next competition, this could be his last chance.

Famously given growth hormones because of a deficiency as a child, he joined Barcelona at the age of 13, because they agreed to pay for his medical treatment.

Seventeen years later, with four hundred appearances under his belt and a record of almost a goal a game, that decision must rate as one of the best in footballing history.

He is Argentina's all time leading goal scorer, but until he wins the biggest cup, whether he can be compared with Maradona, or even Pele, is open to question.

Messi is a great benefactor as well, being heavily associated with good causes supporting vulnerable children. He set up his own charity, the Leo Messi Foundation, again an organization that supports children, and has worked with UNICEF.

In a world where footballers normally dominate the back pages for their skills, and the front for their indiscretions, it is heart-warming to learn of a player who, quietly but effectively, pays back the game by working for those who will never achieve to the levels he has attained.

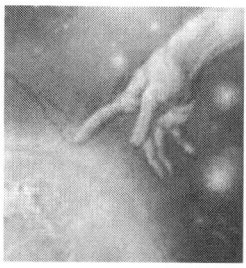

Maradona?

Who Might We know?

Sergio Aguero and Nicolas Otamendi both play for Manchester City, while Manual Lanzini is a key player for West Ham and Sergio Romero is on the books of Manchester United.

Manager: Jorge Sampaoli

Road to the Finals

In the words of the immortal Paul McCartney, it was a long and winding one. After a poor start, no wins from three games, matters picked up with four consecutive victories.

However, consistency was lacking and draws against Venezuela and Peru were followed with defeats to Paraguay and Brazil. The route continued to deviate, with just three points from the next four games, leaving the White and Sky blues needing a victory against Ecuador – step up Mr. Messi.

Prospects

With their good track record and the world's best player in their ranks, the Argentinians are in with a shout. Nevertheless, their poor form in qualifying wasn't just against the big boys, and they are vulnerable at any stage of the competition. Class usually tells, though, and it would be a surprise if they did not make at least the last eight.

Player from the Past: Alfredo Di Stefano

In his obituary from 2014, the Daily Telegraph called Di Stefano the greatest player of all time, bar Pele.

The striker, who led Real Madrid's line to European glory, was a great goal scorer. But more than this, he was a brilliant on field strategist. Under his leadership, he led them to European victory from 1956 to 1960, an astonishing reign, even in those far gone days.

Di Stefano was born into Barracas, a poor area of Argentina's capital, the grandson of an Italian immigrant.

His father was a footballer as well, who played for River Plate. Di Stefano followed in his father's footsteps in 1942, and his renowned short fuse showed itself quickly, when he quit the youth team following a row with his coach.

He moved to play in Colombia following the war, and scored an astonishing 259 goals in 292 games there.

He joined Real Madrid (a controversial move, as he was still officially a River Plate player) and scored a hat trick against Barcelona four days later.

A brilliant passer, with a determination to tackle back, and a fine finisher, he was the archetype of the total footballer that the Dutch would exemplify in the 1970s.

Di Stefano played only seven times for Argentina (he also represented Colombia) before becoming a naturalized Spanish international.

After retiring, he moved into club management, winning the European Cup Winners Cup in 1980, defeating Arsenal on penalties.

Peru

World Cup Pedigree

1930 – First round

1970 – Quarter finals

1978 – Second group stage, fourth of four

1982 – Group stage, fourth of four

Star Player: Farfan

The veteran striker has scored twenty-three times for Peru, and currently represents Lokomotiv Moscow as his club side.

At thirty-three, his pace shows no signs of dropping off, and he scored one of the two goals that saw Peru defeat New Zealand in the play offs.

The Peruvians are not a team glistening with star quality, and Farfan may need to seize the mantle one final time if they are to do well.

Who Might We know?

Only Andre Carrillo plays in the Premier League from those with a chance of making the final cut. The winger is on loan from Benfica, and is turning out for Watford.

Manager: Ricardo Gareco. He is nicknamed 'The Tiger'. Need we say more?

Road to the Finals

With just four points from their opening six games, the chances of Peru making the cut seemed remote.

Things picked up a little after that, but the well fancied Peruvians still had to go through the play offs. They beat New Zealand (that mighty force of world football) 2-0 at home but the long flight did for them on the return, where they struggled to a 0-0 draw.

Prospects

They are ranked tenth in the world, but coming fifth in South America then making hard work of overcoming New Zealand does not augur well.

On seeding, they should progress out of their group stage, but it is hard to see much beyond that.

Their coach might be a 'tiger', but can Peru be more than pussy cats on the pitch?

Player from the Past: Teodoro Fernandez

'Lolo' was a prolific goal scorer, a hero even today at his club Universitario, where he spent his entire career, scoring 156 goals in 180 matches.

He was also a key figure for Peru, scoring two goals for every three appearances in his thirty-two international matches. Like many other greats of his era, his international career and world cup opportunities were curtailed by World War II.

Fernandez was known for his powerful shooting, and was top scorer when Peru won the Copa America.

Colombia

World Cup Pedigree

1962 – Group stage, fourth of four

1990 – Last sixteen

1994 – Group stage, fourth of four

1998 – Group stage, third of four

2014 – Quarter final

Star Player: James Rodriguez

A properly world class player at his best, he not only won the Golden boot at the last World Cup, but has played for both Real Madrid and Bayern Munich.

However, he seems to save his best for his national team, something they will need if they are to progress from the group stages.

Who Might We know?

David Ospina is the back up keeper to Petr Cech at Arsenal, and Davinson Sanchez plays across the way in North London. Jose Izquierdo takes advantage of the warmer south coast at Brighton.

Manager: Jose Pekerman

Road to the Finals

Although they managed just two points from the final three matches, better early form meant that they qualified from the South American group in fourth place.

Prospects

They are ranked thirteenth in the world, according to Fifa, but that seems a tad generous. Nobody will be too surprised if they fail to make their seeding, and go out in the group stage.

Player from the Past: Andres Escobar

Columbia was one of most dangerous places on Earth in the 1990s. Drug lords were all powerful, and gangs ruled the streets. Many areas of the country were 'no-go' for all but locals and gangsters from the right side of town.

Andres Escobar. Bill Shankly once said football was a matter of life and death. It was for Escobar

But if the country was in turmoil, the football team was on the crest of a wave. They had dominated the South American qualification group, and had beaten Argentina 5-0, with several fans killed during the celebrations that followed.

So, they entered the World Cup in the US as one of the favourites. Drawn in a group with the hosts, Romania and Switzerland, qualification seemed inevitable.

But they lost their opening game, and needed something against the US in their second match. With forty-four years since their previous victory, the chance of a shock result for the Americans seemed remote.

But the home side prevailed by two goals to one, with Escobar contributing an own goal.

It later turned out that several Colombian players had received death threats before the competition, and midfielder Gabriel Gomez had refused to participate in the match.

The own goal itself, though, was not untypical of its kind, a low cross into the box with the defender stretching to cut it out.

He makes contact, but cannot control it and the keeper, who has scurried across his goal in anticipation of the ball reaching a USA attacker, cannot readjust, and the balls slides into the goal.

Columbia lose, and exit the tournament. Five days later, Escobar was in a restaurant in his home town of Medellin, which was well known for illegal cocaine business in those days.

Three men, driving the type of off road vehicles common among the drug and gambling cartels, began to argue with him about the own goal, and then shot him.

One witness claimed the words 'Thanks for the own goal,' were uttered.

Later, some US players observed that the Colombians seemed uninterested in the match, and certainly their play was well below par.

Escobar is not the best player to ever represent Colombia, but his tragic and untimely demise has made him one of the most notorious.

Uruguay

World Cup Pedigree

The only team to win the tournament at their first attempt (although, somebody had to win the inaugural event) they went on to win the second finals they reached as well. Sadly, it has been downhill since then.

1930 – Winners

1950 – Winners

1954 – Fourth

1962 – Group stage, third of fourth

1966 – Quarter finals

1970 – Fourth

1974 – Group stage, fourth of four

1986 – Last sixteen

1990 – Last sixteen

2002 – Group stage, third of four

2010 – Fourth

2014 – Last sixteen

Star Player: Luis Suarez

The former Liverpool player's brace was enough to secure qualification in their final group match, which was against Bolivia.

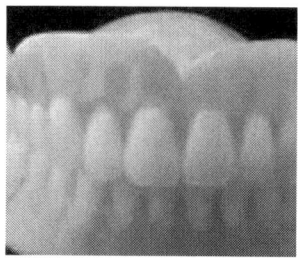

Will Uruguay get their teeth into the competition?

Of course, the Barcelona striker has endured a good degree of controversy, on two occasions being suspended for biting opponents, but at the age of thirty, he seems more disciplined and will offer a serious threat to every defence in the competition.

Who Might We know?

No Premier League players, but Abel Hernandez turns out for Hull.

Manager: Oscar Tabarez, and he has been in charge since 2006, quite an achievement for an international manager.

Road to the Finals

It looked for at least half of the qualifying stages as though Uruguay would come out top of their group, before their own dip in form coincided with Brazil's upsurge.

But a free scoring attack, led by the inimitable Suarez, made a meal of many defences and qualification was assured early on.

Prospects

Must be good. With a strong attack, somewhat dampened by a tendency to let in goals, the Uruguayan's world ranking of seventeenth seems ludicrously low.

A good each way bet for the title, they probably won't win it, but progress to the last eight is highly likely, and from there, anything can happen.

Player from the Past: Hector Castro

When Hector Castro scored the fourth goal in the final of the first ever World Cup, Uruguay's status in the folklore of football was established forever.

It was the eighty ninth minute, the Uruguayans broke away from the siege on their goal, Castro let fly and the Argentinian keeper, diving forlornly, could only see the ball nestle in the net.

Yet something even more astonishing exists about Hector Castro. He is, almost certainly, the only one-armed player to ever play in a World Cup.

Aged 13, he was chopping wood with his father's electric saw when it slipped, amputating his arm. But he used the stump to good measure, aggressively fending off defenders when he jumped for the ball.

The result in that first final led to riots in Buenos Aires and attacks on the winning side's embassy.

Concacaf

Mexico

World Cup Pedigree

1930 – Group stage, fourth of four

1950 – Group stage, fourth of four

Despite the terrible earthquake of 1985, Mexico still hosted the 1986 tournament

1954 – Group stage, fourth of four

1958 – Group stage, fourth of four

1962 – Group stage, third of four

1966 – Group stage, third of four

1970 – Quarter finals

1978 – Group stage, fourth of four

1986 – Quarter finals

1994 – Last sixteen

1998 – Last sixteen

2002 – Last sixteen

2006 – Last sixteen

2010 – Last sixteen

2014 – Last sixteen

Star Player: Raul Jimenez

The Benfica striker is the most expensive player ever from Mexico.

Who Might We know?

Javier Hernandez is often up front for West Ham. Carlos Vela, the former Arsenal striker, is enjoying life with Real Sociedad in Spain.

Manager: Juan Carlos Osorio

Quite a character is Mr. Osorio. Not only is he a graduate from Liverpool's John Moore's University, but he was assistant manager at Manchester City for a spell. He was recently banned for six matches for an aggressive attack on officials. He should manage a bigger world name, he could say what he liked then.

Road to the Finals

Nuclear Physics? Chaos Theory? Concacaf world cup qualification? What is your specialized field? What can be strongly advised is not to go with the third, because little can be more complicated in life.

However, through the mire and the numerous stages what was abundantly clear was that the best team was Mexico. By a mile.

Prospects

They ought to get through their qualifying group, and will be hard to beat. Last sixteen seems a good prediction, but nobody should be surprised if they go further than this.

Player from the Past: Hugo Sanchez

Known in equal measure for his spectacular volleys, lethal strikes in front of girl and tight 1980s perm, Hugo Sanchez is often considered the finest footballer of all time from the Central and North Americas.

He left his homeland for a brief spell in the North American Soccer League, unusually for that league as a player with his future in front of him, rather than behind.

However, it was his time in Madrid, firstly for Atletico, then Real, that secured his name as a great, and remains today one of the leading scorers from La Liga.

He also took part in three World Cups for Mexico. These days, he works in the football media.

Costa Rica

World Cup Pedigree

1990 – Last sixteen

2002 – Group stage, third of four

2006 – Group stage, fourth of four

2014 – Quarter finals

Star Player Keylor Navas

The thirty-year-old goalkeeper has become the number one between the sticks at Real Madrid. The player should be at his peak, aged 31, for the finals and could provide that touch of expertise which gives his nation a chance to stay in matches against better teams.

A committed Christian, he keeps his football in perspective, saying that God is his primary love and motivation in his life.

Who Might We know?

Arsenal striker Joel Campbell is the only Premier League player, and currently he is on loan to the Spanish club, Real Betis. Christian Gamboa plays for Celtic.

Joel Campbell

Manager: Oscar Ramirez, who took over from Paulo Wanchope after he became involved in a mass brawl when the Costa Ricans were playing Panama. It's always interesting in the heat of Central America.

Road to the Finals

Getting comfortably through their fourth-round group, Costa Rica became the draw kings in the final group stage, losing just twice but drawing four times. Given that, they were well off the pace set by Mexico, but stayed just ahead of their rivals from the US, Honduras and Panama.

It was close though.

Prospects

From Pot Three in the draw, there is not much to suggest that they will progress beyond the group stages. They do not concede many, but then do not score that often either, even against weaker opposition.

Goals will therefore be tough as they face a rise in class at the finals, while their defence is more likely to be breached.

Player from the Past: Paulo Wanchope

The much travelled former international saved his best work for his national side, scoring forty-five times in seventy-three matches.

His long limbs and misleading clumsiness gained him cult status, something helped by his debut for Derby County where he scored an astonishing goal in a victory of Manchester Utd. Wanchope dribbled through four players before beating Peter Schmeichel. The goal was voted the best of all time by Derby fans.

Wanchope went on to play for West Ham and Manchester City before continuing his career at six other clubs.

Panama

World Cup Pedigree

This will be Panama's first appearance in the finals. They first entered the competition in 1978, but have not previously made it beyond the qualifying stages.

Star Player: Luis Tejada

The striker is Panama's leading goal scorer of all time, with forty-three goals. He will be thirty-six by the finals, but still represents the team's best chance of creating and scoring goals.

Who Might We know?

Probably none of them, as there are no players likely to make the squad who ply their trade in the UK, although Gabriel Torres is a striker for FC Lausanne.

Manager: Hernan Dario Gomez

Road to the Finals

Panama scraped through. Although their first group stages saw them comfortably see off Haiti and Jamaica (not a huge achievement) they ended up behind Costa Rica, and only gained an automatic place on goal difference. That this was a negative difference says a lot.

Prospects

Can the football team link as well as the canal?

They will find it hard to score, managing just a goal a game in qualification. Only three teams are ranked lower than them (hosts Russia, Saudi Arabia and South Korea) and there is little to suggest they will spring any kind of surprise.

Player from the Past: Jose Mario Torres

The Panama defender played no less than seventy-five times for his country, and never managed a goal.

His loyalty to Panama was demonstrated when he turned down a big move after being asked to take on Honduran nationality to meet foreign player quotas.

He also secured the league title with Sporting San Miguelito in his first season as manager.

Watch this space if the national team needs a new manager.

Africa

Tunisia

World Cup Pedigree

1978 – Group stage, third of four (but in winning their opening game, against Mexico, Tunisia became the first African team to win a match at a finals.)

1998 – Group stage, fourth of four

2002 – Group stage, fourth of four

2006 – Group stage, third of four

Star Player Aymen Abdennour

The defender has worked his way around some strong European teams, including Valencia and Marseille. Given a good showing, one of the rumours linking him with the likes of Watford, Chelsea and Everton might come to fruition.

Who Might We know?

Wahbi Khazri is a Sunderland player, currently on loan in France.

Manager: Nabil Maaloul

A man with a real commitment to Tunisian football. Not only did he win over seventy caps as a player, but he has been assistant manager and is now in his second spell as manager. So distressed was he at the side's failure to qualify in 2014 that he resigned, before returning in April 2017.

Road to the Finals

The CAF qualification features qualifying matches to reduce the number of teams to twenty. These are then divided into five groups of four, and the winner of each group goes through.

Tunisia topped their group a point ahead of DR Congo, winning four and drawing two matches.

Prospects

They are ranked 28th in the world, and were in Pot Three for seeding, but have a chance of going through to the knock out round, but I wouldn't stake a decent pair of socks on it. They would need England and Belgium to slip up to have any chance of progress.

Player from the Past: Ali Boumnijel

The goalkeeper

The Tunisian goalie played fifty-one times for the national team in a spell which covered sixteen years from 1991 to 2007.

In the 2006 World Cup, he was the oldest participant, being aged forty, and represented his country at two earlier World Cups. As such, we think he is the only player to represent his country in three quarters of their World Cup appearances.

He also played in goal for the nation's victorious 2004 African Nations Cup campaign.

He now coaches goalkeeping for the Chinese Football Association.

Egypt

World Cup Pedigree

1934 – Group stage, fourth of four (Egypt became the first African team to participate in a finals)

1990 – Group stage, fourth of four

Star Player Mohamed Salah

The superfast striker will present a problem to all defensive units. He can be a bit hit and miss – reference his unsuccessful spell at Chelsea – but when on song can be one of the most devastating strikers on the planet. His start to the season with Liverpool in 2017 was scintillating.

Who Might We know?

As well as Salah, Mohamed Elneny plays for Arsenal, Ahmed Hegazy is in the Baggies' team and Ramadan Sobhi turns out for Stoke City. Ahmed Elmohamady is still trying to turn Aston Villa back into a proper football team, and Sam Morsy plays for League One Wigan.

Manager: Hector Cuper

On the journey to making history - 1934

Road to the Finals

Egypt qualified comfortably from their group, with just one defeat (away to Uganda).

Prospects

Egypt have some top players and are well organized. They will be difficult to break down in Russia, and in Salah have a striker with the pace and talent to unsettle any defence.

The last sixteen is a definite possibility.

Player from the Past: Mahmoud Mokhtar

The little striker with the giant leap was the most capped player to represent Egypt way back in that 1934 World Cup. He was also the national team's captain.

At the time, he was widely considered to be the greatest Egyptian footballer of all time. In fact, in his eight-year international career, he played only ten matches, scoring nine goals. But this was an era when African football was almost non-existent on the world stage.

He played his entire career in Cairo, representing the Al Ahly side, who have won the Egyptian league no fewer than thirty nine times. The club's stadium is named after it's early star's nickname, el-Tetsh

Senegal

World Cup Pedigree

2002 – Quarter finals

Star Player: Sadio Mane

The Liverpool winger is approaching World Class, and the Reds are only half a team without him. Whether he can take Senegal to a higher level only time and the competition will tell.

Who Might We know?

Cheikhou Kouyate is a West Ham regular, as is Diafra Sakho. Idrissa Gueye plays for Everton.

From the Championship we might recognize Alfred N'Diaye from Wolves and the Birmingham City player Cheikh N'Doye.

Manager: Former Portsmouth and Birmingham City player Aliou Cisse.

Road to the Finals

Senegal qualified with ease from their group, winning four and drawing two of their matches in the final stages.

Prospects

They are a tough team to score against, but probably lack just enough class to get beyond the group stages.

They have no players who are going to cause major worries to higher ranked teams (beyond Sane), although their Premiership players will provide much needed experience.

Player from the Past: Papa Bouba Diop

The player with the name that sounds like a dance craze was a key member of the successful Senegal campaign of 2002, which started with a 1-0 win over the reigning world champions, France.

Papa Diop enjoyed much of his career bestriding the English leagues with the likes of Fulham, Portsmouth, West Ham and, at the end of his career, Birmingham City.

Dancing to glory?

It was at Fulham that he gained the nickname, the Wardrobe, in honour of his massive build and immense strength.

But Papa Diop also played in Europe, notably in Switzerland, France and Greece.

Nigeria

World Cup Pedigree

1994 – Last sixteen

1998 – Last sixteen

2002 – Group stage, fourth of four

2010 – Group stage, fourth of four

2014 – Last sixteen

Star Player – Kelechi Iheanacho

The striker promised much at Manchester City, and it seemed as though Leicester got a really good buy. But the former champions are yet to see the best of the striker. He could well come of age in Russia.

Who Might We know?

On top of the Leicester City striker named above, Wilfred Ndidi and Ahmed Musa are Kingpower Stadium regulars. Alex Iwobi is impressive at Arsenal, and Victor Moses a key member of the Chelsea squad. Ola Aina is a Chelsea player, currently on loan to Hull City.

And the Chelsea link is completed with John Mikel Obi. The former blue is now earning big bucks in China.

Manager: Gernot Rohr

Road to the Finals

Nigeria were the clearest qualifiers from any of the African nations, securing their place by six points (out of just eighteen possible). They were unbeaten, free scoring and defensively mean.

They were also in the toughest group, which included African champions Cameroon and Algeria.

After a few years in the doldrums, this will be the third consecutive World Cup for which the Super Eagles will be flying high.

Prospects

They might be from the fourth pot of seeds, but have enough class to make it to the last sixteen, perhaps beyond.

In fact, a quarter final is not beyond them. We can't see them becoming the first African semi finalists, but it is not impossible.

Player from the Past: Kanu

The long limbed, tricky forward captained the Eagles for sixteen years, played for them for seventeen and earned eighty seven caps, scoring twelve times. He also won an Olympic Gold medal.

His club career was, if anything, more spectacular. With his various clubs he won the Champions League, UEFA Cup, three FA cups and the Premier league. He started his career with Iwuanyanwu Nationale in

Nigeria, before moving to Ajax, Inter Milan and Arsenal.

Sopwell House – a good place for coffee for Arsenal fans.

From there he moved to West Brom and spent six seasons at Portsmouth, where he played 141 times.

A cult figure among fans, he was not just a great player, but is also a great person. He is a UNICEF Goodwill Ambassador.

This writer had the opportunity of observing Kanu on one occasion. This took place at Sopwell House Hotel, near Watford. The Hotel is close to the Arsenal training facilities at London Colney, and the players would meet there of a morning.

I was waiting with my wife to be to discuss our wedding arrangements with the hotel's events organizer – we were to have our reception in the splendid grounds.

The Arsenal players were in the nearby lounge, and would come out one at a time for a short discussion with manager Arsene Wenger and his assistant of those days, Pat Rice. We were sitting at the next table, and could hear the players discussing various matters around fitness with their bosses.

At some point, a boy of about eleven arrived with his father. Both were clearly nervous and eventually the boy asked, very quietly, if he could give his autograph book to someone to get it signed by the gathered players.

There was a bit of a hush, Wenger and Rice were clearly busy and Arsene gave a little embarrassed shrug.

Out stepped Kanu. 'I'll take him, boss' he said, 'and I can show him around.'

The next thing, the happy boy and his overawed father were heading into the lounge.

About forty five minutes later, we had conducted our own meeting and were having an official tour of the hotel. We bumped into Kanu and his party, as he was explaining some signed football shirts hanging in a corridor.

I don't know if he made training that day, but taking the boy on a tour and getting his autograph book filled was a fantastically kind gesture from a world superstar.

Morocco

World Cup Pedigree

1970 – Group stage, fourth of four

1986 – Last sixteen

1994 – Group stage, fourth of four

1998 – Group stage, third of four

Star Player: Mehdi Benatia

Who Might We know?

Sofiane Boufal is well respected at Southampton, and Romain Saiss is a part of the successful Championship outfit at Wolves.

Manager: Herve Renard

A foxy manager who has won the African Cup of Nations twice, once with the powerful Ivory Coast, but also with little Zambia.

He won't be fazed by the big time in Russia, his first job in management was to take the reins at Cambridge United.

Road to the Finals

Their solid defence made them comfortable qualifiers from Group C. In fact, the only goal they conceded was in an earlier knock out match against Equatorial Guinea

Hopefully, this won't be the reaction to Morocco in Russia

Prospects

If you are planning on going to Russia for the finals, and fancy seeing some matches, avoid those involving Morocco. They might have a brilliant defence, not conceding a goal in any of their six group games, but they failed to score in three of those matches themselves.

The group stages will represent the limit of their achievements.

Player from the Past: Ezzaki Badou

Badou was the captain, and goalkeeper of the 1986 World Cup Moroccan team who surprised everyone by topping their group.

That did them little favour, because they met eventual runners up West Germany in the last 16.

The Moroccan progress was made on the back of some tremendous defending. Two 0-0 draws and a 3-1 victory over Portugal saw them triumphant, but in the last 16 match Ezzaki Badou had the game of his life.

The Africans held out until the 87th minute when the heroic keeper was eventually beaten by a Lothar Matthaus free kick.

His performances earned the keeper a transfer to Mallorca, in Spain, where he played for six years. Following retirement from playing, he moved into club and international management, taking on the national team on two occasions.

Asia/Oceania

Iran

World Cup Pedigree

1978 – Group stage, fourth of four

1998 – Group stage, third of four

2006 – Group stage, fourth of four

2014 – Group stage, fourth of four

Star Player: Sardar Azmoun

Linked from time to time with Liverpool, the twenty-two year old is considered by those in the know perhaps the most talented player to ever emerge from the Middle East.

Who Might We know?

Umm, nobody.

Manager: None other than much travelled and assistant to Sir Alex Ferguson, Carlos Queiroz.

The ex-Man U man might be making this anguished gesture a lot

Road to the Finals

Qualification through the Asian/Oceania group involves a knock out competition for the smaller nations, leading to a group stage into which the bigger teams join. Qualifiers from this stage move into two groups for final qualification. The top two of each group go through automatically.

The two third place teams play off, and the winner has a final play off with the fourth placed team from Concacaf.

Iran were dominant throughout their groups, winning six and drawing four matches to win qualifying group A.

Prospects

Ranked thirty fourth, they are the only team from this qualifying department to avoid Pot Four in the draw.

Having said that, there isn't much chance of any further progression.

Player from the Past: Karim Bagheri

The powerhouse defensive midfielder was a regular scorer for the Iranian national team, and participated in their most successful campaign, the 1998 World Cup.

What marked Bagheri out was that, in a time when Iran's players were very much home based, he was playing in Germany. In fact, he was the only player not plying his trade in Iran at the time.

Bagheri was even signed for a British club, Charlton Athletic, who were experiencing a golden period under Alan Curbishley. Unfortunately, he was injured throughout most of his time there, and played just fifteen minutes, against Ipswich.

However, he made an impression on the English manager, who felt he would have been very successful as a deep lying midfielder who could score goals, especially with long shots and from set pieces.

Following retirement, he entered coaching, mostly with his long-time club side, Persepolis.

Australia

World Cup Pedigree

1974 – Group stage, fourth of four

2006 – Last sixteen

2010 – Group stage, third of four

2014 – Group stage, fourth of four

Star Player: Matthew (Maty) Ryan

The Brighton keeper is in fine form as the team from the South Coast continue to exceed expectations in the Premier League. If he can transfer that form into the finals, he might just give Australia a chance of picking up a point of two.

The player is gaining in experience and confidence, and although his domestic season will be a constant challenge, as a player he will only get better.

Who Might We know?

Matthew Ryan (see above) plays for Brighton, and Aaron Mooy for Huddersfield. Jay Federici is at Bournemouth, alongside Brad Smith.

Tom Rogic is a Celtic man, and Bailey Wright (Bristol City), Jackson Irvine (Hull), Massimo Luongo (QPR) and Mile Jedinak (Aston Villa) represent Antipodeans in the Championship.

Former Everton midfielder Tim Cahill remains a pivotal figure in the national side, despite entering the latter part of his thirties.

Still directing things – Tim Cahill

Manager: The last one resigned after the stress of qualifying. As long as they don't take Eddie Jones...

Road to the Finals

Australia had to go through two play offs – firstly against Syria and then Honduras – to reach this stage.

Prospects

They have players with top league experience and could defy their odds and scrape through to the last sixteen, but it is an outside chance.

Player from the Past: Harry Kewell

Kewell had a highly successful time with Leeds United, when they were a strong Premiership outfit, and Liverpool.

He was named young player of the year, and helped guide the Elland Road team to the semi-finals of the Champions League.

Along with fellow Leeds United Aussie Mark Viduka, he played for his nation during their strongest years, and gained many plaudits.

He moved to Liverpool, but under unfortunate circumstances. England's Gary Lineker claimed that a large percentage of the transfer fee went to Kewell's unregistered agent. That was, said Lineker, how the club had secured the player's services amid offers from Arsenal, Chelsea, Manchester United, Milan and Barcelona.

It is a measure of the high esteem with which the Aussie was regarded that he attracted such clubs.

He won the Champions League with Liverpool, but it was during his poorest season in England. In fact, it turned out later that he was suffering from a long-term groin injury.

When Kewell retired from playing he went into football management, and is currently in charge of the second division club, Crawley Town. His combative came to the fore soon after his appointment, as he rowed with fans who were being abusive towards him. Fair enough, most would agree.

Japan

World Cup Pedigree

1998 – Group stage, fourth of four

2002 – Last sixteen

Leicester were 5000-1 for the Premiership, Japan just 250-1 for the World Cup. Can Okazaki do it again?

2006 – Group stage, fourth of four

2010 – Last sixteen

2014 – Group stage, fourth of four

Star Player: Shinji Okazaki

There are some talented forwards in the Japanese squad, but the seasoned head of Leicester's Okazaki just pushes him to the top of the list.

The player was crucial in the Foxes League title winning team, bringing the best out of star man Jamie Vardy. A couple of seasons on, although Okazaki starts less often, many pundits believe his ability to link play and work hard has not been replaced in the side, and he should start every game.

Surely, he will for Japan.

Who Might We know?

Keisuke Honda?? Shinji Kagawa?? Takuma Asano has turned heads at Arsenal, but not enough to prevent him being loaned to Stuttgart. Maya Yoshida is a Southampton player.

Manager: Vahid Halilhodzic, although rumours suggest that his time could be limited. If there is a change before publication, we will add it below!

Road to the Finals

Japan won Group B of the final qualification group, finishing just above Saudi Arabia and Australia.

A shock defeat at home to the UAE was followed by more consistent performances.

Prospects

Although ranked forty fourth in the world, Japan have the best chance of getting out of their group of any team from this part of the competition. A mean defence allied to some good players, plus a climate they will enjoy, means that they have a small chance of progression.

Player from the Past: Shinji Ono

Tensai (meaning 'genius') is the player many consider to be the greatest Asian footballer of all time.

At 38, he is still playing, turning out for the J1 club Consadole Sappora.

He played for Japan in every World Cup from 1998 to 2010, although was injured for the tournament in 2006, still playing though in the qualifiers.

A sharp passer with a clear vision of the game, Ono won 56 caps for Japan and played for Feyenoord for five seasons.

Injury blighted what might have been his best years, and he missed competitions between 2003 and 2007, but as retirement comes closer he remains close to the heart of Japanese supporters.

South Kora

World Cup Pedigree

1954 – Group stage, fourth of four

Up for the Cup? Can the Koreans improve on 1954?

1986 – Group stage, fourth of four

1990 – Group stage, third of four

1998 – Group stage, fourth of four

2002 – Fourth

2006 – Group stage, third of four

2010 – Last sixteen

2014 – Group stage, fourth of four

Star Player: Song Heung-min.

The Tottenham man recovered well from a fractured arm, earned playing for South Korea in their qualifier against Qatar last summer.

While Harry Kane generally keeps him out of the Tottenham team, he often comes on as a sub, and has a good scoring record for his team with a scoring rate of one in three or better. He is also higher up the pecking order than the experienced ex Swansea player Fernando Llorente.

Song will bring a touch of class to the hard-working South Korean national side.

Who Might We know?

Alongside the Spurs striker, Ki Sung-yueng of Swansea is the other Premier league representative.

Manager: Shin Tae-yong (Apparently nicknamed the Asian Mourinho, although we are not quite sure why.)

Road to the Finals

Finishing just a couple of points above both Syria and Uzbekistan, the South Koreans came second in their group. They don't score many goals, but then again, they are quite tight at the back. Not though, when it comes to the higher standard of opposition they will meet at the finals.

Prospects

Even with their Premiership players, it is hard to see the sixty second ranked team in the world getting enough points to get out of their group.

Player from the Past: Yoo Sang-chul

Who can forget the South Korean's unbelievable march to the semi-finals in 2002? They beat Portugal and Poland on their advance to group winners, only dropping points against the eventual runners up in the group, the USA.

Who might have envisaged a group that ended South Korea, USA, Portugal and. Lastly. Poland? Then came the remarkable 2-1 victory over Italy, followed by a penalty victory over Spain in the quarter finals.

Even in the semis, the mighty Germany could only squeeze past them 1-0.   They ended up with a prize of sorts, named the Most Entertaining Team.

The power behind that team was Yoo Sang Chul. A dominating midfield who could win the ball and immediately set his team going forward scored against Poland, but more than this drove his side on in their remarkable run.

He was named in the team of the tournament (along with fellow Korean Hong Myung-bo) and only after the competition did he reveal that he was, in fact, blind in one eye.

For a player also renowned for his ability in the air, that was another astonishing discovery.

Saudi Arabia

World Cup Pedigree

1994 – Last sixteen

1998 – Group stage, fourth of four

2002 – Group stage, fourth of four

2006 – Group stage, fourth of four

Star Player Ummm. If he makes it, Nasser Al Shamrani was the 2014 Asian player of the year. But he has a reputation for losing his rag, once being banned for eight matches after spitting at and headbutting an opponent when his team lost.

Who Might We know?

Sadly, nobody. (Unless Saudi Arabian football is a passion). Mohammed Al Sahlawi has been banging them in, including a hat trick in their qualifying match against Timor Leste, and five in the recent return leg, where the Saudi Arabians hit double figures. Mind you, Timor Leste are not, you might be surprised to hear, a world power when it comes to football. They are ranked 196th in the world, although their population is nearly four times that of Iceland.

Manager: The coach who took the team to the finals, Bert van Marwijk, resigned after qualification and has been replaced by Edgardo Bauza. He lasted for just a couple of months and his five matches in charge (all friendlies) saw two wins and three defeats, although none were hammerings. At the time of writing, no replacement had been announced.

The black gold of oil; but no medal possible.

Road to the Finals

Coming in second in their final group, just above Australia gave the Saudi Arabians their chance to play in Russia. They finished just a point below the winners, Japan.

Prospects

The hosts apart, the lowest ranked team in the competition (sixty-third) should look to enjoy themselves. They should not expect much more.

Player from the Past: Mohamed Abd Al-Jawad

The 'flying wing' was entering the twilight of his long international career by the time of the Saudi Arabian first, and most successful, foray into the World Cup Finals.

The short but dynamic defender, more of a wing back in today's parlance, was 31 and had over a hundred caps to his name by the arrival of the tournament.

Like the remainder of the team, he played his club football in his homeland.

After his career as a player ended, he moved into work as a football agent.

The Most Important Things About Every Finals – Pre-War

From Pickles the Dog to the mystery surrounding Ronaldo (the Brazilian one), the World Cup seems to attract the strange and mysterious.

In this and the following chapters we look at some of the weirder events that have happened at the various tournaments, as well as any other surprising facts and dubious practices, something with which the competition has been rather too closely associated over the years...

1930 – Uruguay

Final - Uruguay 4 – 2 Argentina

Semi Finals - Argentina 6 – 1 United States

Uruguay 6 – 1 Yugoslavia

Third Place - Yugoslavia/United States

This was the only World Cup without a play off. Apparently, Yugoslavia had a strop following the refereeing of the semi-final, and refused to play in one.

However, in 1984, an erroneous bulletin was issued by Fifa, implying that there had been a game, which was won by Yugoslavia, 3-1.

'It's my ball so I'll decide who plays.' At one point, it looked as though the final was in doubt when neither side could decide who should provide the ball. In the end, the organizers ruled that the first half would be played with an Argentinian ball, and the second with one from Uruguay.

An unlikely hero of the tournament was the US coach. Rushing on to treat an injured player, he tripped, dropped the bottle of chloroform (yes, that's right) he was carrying, breathed in the fumes and promptly knocked himself out.

France's Captain died in 1944 – Alex Villaplane was executed for collaborating with the occupying Germans.

Interfering club owners eat your hearts out, the Romanian team was selected by their King, Carol II.

And in the Argentina v Mexico match, the referee was the manager of Bolivia, and he had the coach of Romania as one of his linesmen.

1934 – Italy

Final – Italy 2 – 1 Czechoslovakia

Semi-Finals – Italy 1-0 Austria

Czechoslovakia 3-1 Germany

Third Place – Germany 3-2 Austria

The concept of qualification was created for the 1934 World Cup, as there had been none for the previous tournament.

For the 1930 competition, participation had been through invitation and with only four European clubs willing to travel to South America, the hosts got the hump and refused to defend their title in Italy.

We might moan, with justification, that the FA are narrow minded and inward looking, but they have at least moved forwards from their member, Charles Sutcliffe. His views on the home nations' lack of participation were explained thus. *'The national association of England, Scotland, Wales and Ireland have quite enough to do in their own international championship, which seems to me a far better World (!!!!) Championship than the one to be staged in Rome.'* So, there you go, Italy, you only won because England were too good to take part. Yah sucks.

Something that could not happen today (cough, cough), the competition was seized upon for political means, with Benito Mussolini seeking to use the tournament as a chance to promote his brand of fascism. The final was played in the neutrally named Stadium of the National Fascist Party.

1938 – France

Final – Italy 4-2 Hungary

Semi-Finals – Hungary 5-1 Sweden

Italy 2-1 Brazil

Third Place – Brazil 4-2 Sweden

Italy are the only team to win the trophy twice with the same coach – the master tactician is Vittorio Pozzo

Yet more bad feeling erupted between Europe and South America. The Latin continent had believed that the competition would alternate between continents, but Europe was having none of that.

Indeed, there were a number of high profile absentees, even from qualification. Spain was banned, because it was at war. Uruguay and Argentina refused to take part because they thought the tournament should be held in South America.

This was a bit harsh on Europe, who were quite prepared to open their tournament up; two teams from South America were involved, and even one from Asia (although that was the Dutch East Indies, can't have teams from Asia them taking part without European colonizers could we?) So, the 1938 competition was a genuine World Event, with 11 teams from Europe, and three not.

As a tournament, it marked a watershed. The Netherlands would not reappear for 36 years, Norway for 56. Cuba would never be represented again. The Dutch East Indies would not only never play in another World Cup, but would also disappear as a country, re-emerging as Indonesia.

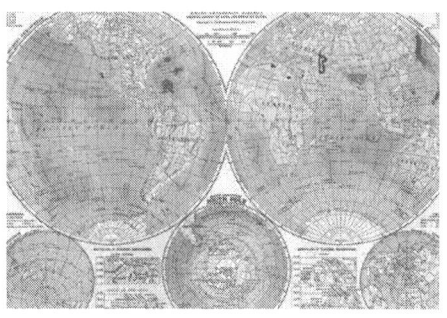

It was a different world back then

With the intervention of World War II, Italy would become the longest continuous holders of the title,

World Champions, since there would not be another tournament for twelve years.

They Think It's All Over…– 1950-66

1950 – Brazil

Final Uruguay 2-1 Brazil

Semi Finals – Brazil 6-1 Spain

Uruguay 3-2 Sweden

Third Place – Sweden 3-1 Spain

The last four actually played in a group for this competition, although the key games are printed above. It was the only time that a proper final was not played.

For the first time, the trophy was called the Jules Rimet Cup, the Fifa president's twenty fifth anniversary of taking charge being honored with the name.

Finding a host nation was difficult, with most of Europe in ruins and economies devastated. Eventually, Brazil stepped forward with a similar bid to the one they had made for the abandoned 1942 competition. The defending champions, Italy, had no chance of retaining the cup as many of their squad had been killed in the Superga air crash the year before.

The Battle of Santiago

The FA in the UK once again covered themselves with glory. They agreed to participate only if their qualifying group was the previous year's home international series.

England won, and Scotland came second. Both qualified. However, the Scottish chairman of the SFA, George Graham, refused to let the team travel as they had come second.

At the last minute, India also withdrew. The reasons given were financial, but many felt that the banning of barefoot players was behind the decision. At the time, Indian footballers played barefoot. My father had first hand experience of this. In the late 1940s he was on the sub-continent doing his National Service.

A touring side of English professionals and internationals visited his region, and was due to play the Indian national team, when the English goalkeepers went down with stomach complaints. As the regimental 'keeper, my Dad was drafted in.

The English were well and truly thrashed, and my Dad would often tell of the power of the Indian's shooting, with their feet bare.

One of the biggest shocks in World Cup history occurred when Joe Gaetjens scored for the USA to beat England.

Gaetjens came from Haiti, and returned there after retirement, setting up a successful dry cleaning business. But when 'Papa Doc' Duvalier was elected to power, the country turned into one of the most despotic in world history. People disappeared, were tortured, were stolen from their beds at night.

The footballer's family were politically orientated, and left the country, but Gaetjens was simply a former footballer who had made good in business. He decided to stay, but shortly after Duvalier decided that elections were not a good thing, and declared himself the country's lifelong President, Gaetjens was arrested.

He was never seen again. Eight years later his death was officially reported, although most believed he had been murdered within days of his abduction.

1954 – Switzerland

Final – West Germany 3-2 Hungary

Semi Finals – West Germany 6-1 Austria

Hungary 4-2 Uruguay

Third Place – Austria 3-1 Uruguay

Hungary, the Magyars, were by far the best team in the world in 1954, and were expected to triumph. Along with a number of other stars, they had the best player in the world in Ferenc Puskas.

In a precursor to the final, West Germany played the Magyars, and Puskas was injured by Werner Liebrich, the German defender. Although he managed to play in the final, he was clearly unfit and hardly able to run.

The Miracle of Bern, the final match in which West Germany provided a shock result, was full of controversy. Firstly, the German equalizer came about following the clearest of fouls on the Hungarian keeper; secondly Puskas equalized at the end of the game, but the goal was disallowed for offside, although the player was clearly onside.

Finally, allegations of doping emerged after the tournament. Allegedly, the German players were injected with a needle take from the Soviets. Their supposed half time boost was either of Vitamin C or an enhancement drug, methamphetamine. That several players went down with jaundice after the competition adds to the controversial theory.

This tournament provided a magnificent spectacle on the pitch, with the highest scoring team in one competition (Hungary, 27 – they also scored the highest ever average goals per game, with 5.4 and the highest goal difference with a score of +17). There was an average of over five goals per game throughout the tournament. When Austria beat

Switzerland 7-5, that became (and still is) the highest number of goals scored in a single match.

Not a tournament for goalkeepers.

The winning Germans were all amateurs, as there was still no professional league in Germany following the war, and their opponents were amateur by virtue of their being from a country which did not allow professional sports players.

This was the first World Cup to be televised.

1958 – Sweden

Final – Brazil 5-2 Sweden

Semi Finals - Sweden 3-1 West Germany

Brazil 5-2 France

Third Place - France 6-3 West Germany

This was the only World Cup where all four home nations took part.

Qualification looked remarkably straightforward for one nation. Israel won their group without scoring a goal, or kicking a ball. Their opponents in qualification, Turkey, Indonesia and Sudan (a bit of travel involved there) refused to take part. However, Fifa decided that they could not qualify without playing, as it would bring the competition into disrepute (something we know Fifa would never allow). They were told to play Wales, who had finished second in their qualification group. The men from the valleys won.

With the cold war at its height, Fifa decided to avoid any chance of a difficult East and West clash. Rather than seeding the groups, they decided that each would have one British home nation, one team from Western Europe and one from Eastern Europe. The final side would come from the Americas. Asia and Africa were not represented. After all, it was the World Cup.

Just Fontaine, the French striker, secured the highest ever return of goals in a single tournament. Thirteen in six matches. Some distance behind in second, with six, was a young Brazilian who went by the name of Pele.

1962 - Chile

Final - Brazil - 3-1 Czechoslovakia

Semi Finals – Chile 2-4 Brazil

Yugoslavia 1-3 Czechoslovakia

Third Place - Chile 1-0 Yugoslavia

The infamous Battle of Santiago occurred early in the tournament. It was fueled by an astonishingly antagonist article by two Italian journalists, Antonio Ghirelli and Corrado Pizzinelli. Among the accusations made against the host country, and especially its capital Santiago were:

- The phones don't work
- The taxies were as rare as 'faithful husbands'
- Santiago was a 'backwater dump'
- Its people were illiterate alcoholics
- Santiago was full of prostitutes
- The people were proud of its misery and backwardness
- The organization of the tournament was non-existent.

The journalists were forced to flee the country. The Chilean press reacted by publishing stories which described Italians as over-sexed drug addicts.

Against a background where the Italian team's savagery was becoming legendary, and bad feeling between teams was ever present, the game got underway.

It has to be said that English referee Ken Aston struggled with maintaining order on the pitch. He did not seem especially even handed in his dealing with trouble, but perhaps, given the volatility in the crowd, he had issues bigger than a football match to consider.

Having said that, the legendary English commentator, David Coleman, called the game the most 'stupid, appalling, disgusting and disgraceful' match ever seen. Paraphrasing the Chilean motto 'by reason or by force' he said that the Chileans were prepared to be reasonable, but the Italians were only willing to use force.

Check the highlights out on YouTube, they are quite astonishing.

After just five minutes, a savage tackle from behind is made by an Italian, the Chilean kicks out and a mini brawl develops. On twelve minutes, the Italian Ferrini is dispossessed, and has a wild swinging kick at his Chilean tackler, he is sent off. The Italian refused to leave, until a dozen long coated police escort him from the pitch.

A little later Sanchez turns near the corner flag and slips. David, the Italian defender kicks him hard, twice. Sanchez lays him out cold with a left hook. The linesman is just a couple of yards away but neither player is sent off.

Shortly after the two clash again, when David leaps into the air as the Chilean heads the ball, and kicks him full in the face. The Italian is sent off, although wins gold at the next Olympics in the gymnastics event.

Early in the second half, the Chilean's take the lead with a header, but the Italian number 11 tries to stop him with a kung fu kick to the chest.

Later, the site of Ken Aston wrestling two players apart on the ground is somewhat unbecoming. He is like an overactive father physically separating two angry toddlers.

At the end of the game, the Italian Number 7 goes behind the referee, clapping loudly and sarcastically, before shouting insultingly at him. Another mass brawl starts on the pitch.

Ken Aston would gain fame for something slightly more positive later – he would go on to invent the Red and Yellow card system.

The organization of the tournament was set back when the world's worst ever earthquake hit the country in 1960. Most experts declared that it was madness to try to go ahead with the competition, but Chile decided to do so.

1966 – England

Final – England 4-2 (aet) West Germany

Semi Finals – England 2-1 Portugal

West Germany 2-1 Soviet Union

Third Place – Portugal 2-1 Soviet Union

Was it in?

One of the world cup matches due to be played at Wembley clashed with a greyhound meet. It was the football that had to give way. The match moved to the White City Stadium, which had been built nearly fifty years previously to host the 1908 Olympics.

There were once again no African nations at the event. The teams were deeply angered by Fifa's decision that, following their own qualification events, their best teams would need to play off against other group winners. In the end, the entire continent chose to withdraw from qualification.

Only two teams attempted to qualify from the continents of Australasia and Asia – they played off and that was how North Korea got to perform at the finals.

England's victory was greeted by the waving of Union flags rather than the red cross on white of St George.

Immediately after the final whistle, as the England team were celebrating in the changing rooms, a young policeman (Peter Weston) was charged with removing the cup for safe keeping, and replacing it with a replica. He had to grab it from Nobby Stiles, who later claimed that he had no idea of what was going on.

And most famously of all, the Jules Rimet Trophy was stolen before the tournament. It had been on display at an exhibition in London when it was nabbed. A dog named Pickles discovered and went on to become a canine film star.

Another non-human star was World Cup Willie, who became the first ever world cup mascot.

Brilliant Brazil, Total Football and Tight Shorts – 1970-1982

1970 – Mexico

Final – Brazil 4-1 Italy

Semi Finals – Uruguay 1-3 Brazil

Italy 4-3 (aet) West Germany

Third Place – Uruguay 0-1 West Germany

A little personal grouch first, 1970 saw the first Panini sticker books come onto the market. I collected, with the help of my dad, religiously, sending away for those I could not collect. I do remember being disappointed that the England squad seemed larger than the others, which I saw as unfair, until I realized that the names of the players did not necessarily relate to the final groups that were picked.

I distinctly remember completing El Salvador first, and have held a special fondness for the country ever since, although their only other qualification came in 1982.

We even had a neatly presented (filled in by Dad) list of every result, a page cut from a newspaper pull out and folded tidily in the back.

Thanks, Sis!

An immaculate copy would now set one back upwards of £5000; unfortunately, my sister threw my copy out when my bedroom was 'converted' into a store room some years after I left home. We are still not talking.

The 1970 finals were played at high altitude. And in high temperatures. However, the competition saw a return to more attacking football after the growth of defensive play during the 1960s and a good goal per game ratio was earned, one which has not been bettered in subsequent competitions – so a bit of a challenge there to teams in Russia.

This was the first World Cup to be broadcast in colour. It was also the last time for a while that the hosts would play the opening match of the tournament. That honour would switch to the holders, although Russia are playing the opening match in 2018.

As Cup holders, England did little to earn the support of locals, who saw them as cold and xenophobic. Perhaps the arrest of their captain Bobby Moore on false charges of theft in Colombia made them wary. They could not have been happy about being drawn in a group that also included favourites Brazil – there was no seeding. It was in this game that Gordon Banks made what many still consider the greatest ever save, leaping across his goal to send Pele's perfect header away from the net.

Further bad luck though, would haunt the holders when the said Gordon Banks went down with food poisoning before their quarter final against West Germany. Replacement Peter Bonetti made a mistake which allowed the Germans back into a game in which they had been trailing badly.

Following Ken Aston's initiative, this was the first World Cup to employ red and yellow cards, but the red ones stayed in the refs' pockets – not one player was sent off.

1974 – West Germany

Final – Netherland 1-2 West Germany

Semi Final – for this competition, the finalists were the winners of two final groups, with the third and fourth place play off being fought between the second placed teams.

Third Place – Brazil 0-1 Poland

This tournament saw a new trophy, with the Jules Rimet Cup now held for ever by the three times winners, Brazil. The replacement was creatively named the Fifa World Cup trophy, and was sculpted by an Italian, Silvio Gazzaniga.

The Soviet Union refused to travel to Chile for the second leg of their qualification play off, and were banned from the competition.

Zaire became only the second African team to reach the finals, but they did not do too well. They lost 9-0 to Yugoslavia, the joint record defeat (When El

Salvador were beaten 10-1 in 1982, at least they managed a goal)

The first red card was issued at a World Cup finals. It was awarded, perhaps appropriately given the Battle of Santiago which inspired the adoption, to Carlos Caszely of Chile.

It was the first World Cup that the Dutch concept of 'total football' was seen. This style of play dispensed with specialist positions, other than the goalkeeper, with every player adopting the role they needed to play at that particular point during a match. It had been created by Ajax.

Surprise qualifiers Haiti were largely hammered, but Italian goalkeeping legend Dino Zoff's astonishing

1142 minute run without conceding was ended by the island's team.

With the Cold War at one of its most tense points, the group one clash between East and West Germany promised to be explosive. Rather like the Cold War it did not result in all out conflict, with the East team beating the West by 1-0.

The final saw the first penalties to be awarded in a World Cup final. The referee was Englishman Jack Taylor and the first occurred before the German's had touched the ball.

The second was controversial following a spectacular dive (was there contact?), but even more outrageous (or brave, if you support the viewpoint) was the comment from Fifa President Joao Havelange, who claimed that both this, and the 1966 World Cup won by England, had been fixed.

1978 – Argentina

Final – Argentina 3-1 Netherlands

Semi-Finals – There were no semi-finals; the winners of each group went through to the final.

Third Place – Brazil 2-1 Italy

Controversy occurred within Argentina even before a ball had been kicked. The competition logo was based on a famous image of its President, Juan Peron, standing with his hands open and raised.

But then a military coup saw Peron ousted, and the military junta leading the country tried to get the image changed. But the tournament was imminent, in commercial terms, and the country was threatened with enormous lawsuits if they changed the logo. The leadership backed down.

Further problems occurred during the second group stage. Argentina were playing Peru, and needed to win by four goals to reach the final of the tournament. They won 6-0. Many third parties argued that the result had been fixed.

All kinds of arguments were put forward. A Colombian drug lord said that the Peru team had been bribed. A Peruvian politician claimed the result had been arranged as a part of a deal to get some dissidents, living in Argentina, returned to Peru. Another argument said a large supply of grain had been sent to Peru, and a bank account unfrozen. In Brazil, attention was drawn to the Argentinian background of the Peru keeper.

However, no further evidence was found to support the claims.

Another English referee was embroiled in controversy. Clive Thomas awarded a corner to Brazil, when they were playing Sweden. The score was 1-1 and the game was almost over. In fact, it was more than almost over. As the corner was kicked, Thomas blew the final whistle, just as Zico headed the ball directly into the net.

Following later results, it meant that Brazil missed out on heading their first-round group, giving them a tougher draw in the second.

France, for the only time, played in a green and white striped kit. They turned up to play Hungary, to discover that both teams had only their all white strip. The kick off was delayed while the officials sought kit from a local club. Personally, I think that one side should have played in skins, or coats if it was cold. That's how we used to do it, when growing up.

1982 – Spain

Final – Italy 3-1 West Germany

Semi Finals – Poland 0-2 Germany

West Germany 3-3 (aet, 5-4 on penalties) France

Third Place – Poland 3-2 France

This World Cup was one of shocks. The holders lost the opening game of the competition 1-0 to little Belgium, and then the mighty West Germany were due to play African first timers, the minnows of Algeria.

With a touch of unbecoming arrogance, so confident were the Germans of victory that one player said, 'We will dedicate our seventh goal to our wives, and the eighth to our dogs.' The manager promised to get on the first train back to Munich should they lose.

But they underestimated the commitment, passion and sheer quality of the African side. Algeria won 2-1, possibly the most unexpected result in the history of the competition.

Algeria went on to lose to Austria and beat Chile, which meant that they would become the first team from Africa to progress beyond the first round. The only thing that could stop them was a 1-0 or 2-0 win for Germany, in their final match which was against Austria. In that case, both teams would progress at the expense of the Africans. Germany scored early on, and effectively the game ended, with hardly a tackle or serious shot from that point onwards. The Austrian commentator was so appalled that he told his audience to turn off their TVs, and said not a word for the final thirty minutes.

The head of the Austrian delegation at the tournament, Hans Tschak, demonstrated that racism was thriving. His words are astonishing. 'Naturally today's game was played tactically,' he said, 'But if 10000 sons of the desert here in the stadium want to trigger a scandal because of this it just goes to show that they have too few schools.'

We know a bigger joker than even these two

But Algeria got the last laugh. Immense pressure was put on Fifa to take action against the alleged cheats, but surprisingly, they opted to do nothing. However, Algeria can claim the credit for ensuring that final matches are played simultaneously to avoid such an outrage from occurring again.

The tournament saw El Salvador concede double figures, to Hungary (their second nine goal win – they beat South Korea 9-0 in the 1954 finals.

The competition also saw the first ever penalty shoot-out. A bizarre second group stage saw Germany and France meet in the semi-finals. The score was 1-1 when the dreadful tackle on Battiston took place, and the game went into extra time with the French scoring twice. But the Germans fought back and equalized. Inevitably, they won the shoot-out.

When Italy were victorious against the extremely unpopular Germans, Dino Zoff became, at 40, the oldest ever player to win the cup, and Italy became the first team to win the tournament having progressed through the first group stage without winning a match.

The Hand of God and All That 1986-1994

1986 – Mexico

Final – Argentina 3-2 Germany

Semi-Finals - West Germany 2-0 France

Argentina 2-0 Belgium

Third Place – France 4-2 Belgium

The Hand of God and the best World Cup goal ever, not just in the same tournament, not just in the same match but by the same player. Villain one minute, rising to punch the ball home against England. How the referee could possibly miss such a blatant offence? Difficult to answer that one. But the maestro later produced a weaving, mazy run, leaving English players in his wake to score the goal of all time in finals.

Hands featured elsewhere for the first time, and probably in as equally annoying way, as the crowds produced the Mexican wave.

The tournament was originally planned to be held in Colombia, but they could not meet the financial obligations of running the competition. Mexico got it with just three years' notice, then an earthquake in 1985 put the tournament once more in doubt.

1990 – Italy

Final – West Germany 1-0 Argentina

Semi Finals – Argentina 1-1 (aet, 4-3 on penalties) Italy

England 1-1 (aet, 3-4 on penalties) West Germany

Third Place - Italy 2-1 England

Perhaps the most boring World Cup in history, climaxed with a tedious final which sent neutrals reaching for the off button on their televisions. It is easy to forget this in England, because of the nation's second best ever performance.

The competition had the lowest number of goals per game – just 2.21 on average, and, at the time, the most sending offs.

It was not just the players, though, whose disciplinary records were a cause for concern. Margaret Thatcher's loathing for football supporters saw England's group matches all played on the island of Sicily, in Cagliari. The sports minister, Colin Moynihan, made negative remarks about English fans a week before the tournament and this led to frightening levels of security. Certainly, there were many football fans who brought the game into disrepute in those days, Heysel and Hillsborough were still making headlines, but there were also many who were decent folk wanting to enjoy a festival of football.

It never, of course, occurred to Margaret Thatcher that her own policies might have contributed to the hooliganism from which British football was suffering.

During England's quarter final with the emerging Cameroon side, striker Gary Lineker famously suffered the effects of a dodgy stomach, losing, uh, control following a tackle. With true British grit he went on to complete the game.

English disappointment. Gazza couldn't have given more.

1994 – USA

Final – Brazil 0-0 (aet, 3-2 on penalties) Italy

Semi Finals – Sweden 0-1 Brazil

Bulgaria 1-2 Italy

Third Place – Sweden 4-0 Bulgaria

The US, of all the countries to have hosted the World Cup, is the one where football is least supported. Notwithstanding this, financially the 1994 competition was the most successful ever, in fact, it still is. An average attendance of almost 70000 gave credit to the land of plenty. Plenty of fans, in this case.

Since they had first deemed to participate, this was the first tournament at which there were no representatives from the United Kingdom although the Republic of Ireland, under care of Uncle Jack

Charlton, represented the British Isles (and many other nations, given the diversity of the 'qualification criteria' applied to players of the Greens).

The tournament saw Maradona's career end in disgrace, after he was banned for taking a prohibited drug. It was also the tournament where Andres Escobar scored the own goal that led to his death, most probably at the hands of drug barons.

Certainly, the tournament featured some exciting games – remember the bludgeoning brilliance of the Bulgarians, led by the never smiling Hristov Stoichkov? It was also the tournament where the oldest player ever appeared on a World Cup final pitch – the 42 year old Roger Milla of Cameroon.

As we all have probably noticed, the USA is pretty big, and the organizers were keen to show off the tournament to as many regions as possible. This meant journeys of thousands of miles between fixtures, often crossing two or three time zones.

As well as the mental pressure caused by the travelling, most of the matches were played in extreme heat and humidity, with used chilled water packets strewn over pitches by the end of matches.

The opening ceremony featured singer Diana Ross. As a gimmick, she was supposed to kick a ball into a goal with such force that the goal broke into two. Unfortunately, her shot missed the target by some distance, but with the premise that the show must go on, the posts split anyway.

One group in the competition, E, caused the organizers problems when all four teams finished on the same number of points – the only time this has happened. Norway missed out on qualification to the next round with the fewest goals scored.

Battered by the Blatter Years 1998-Present

1998 – France

Final – France 3-0 Brazil

Semi Finals – Brazil 1-1 (aet, 4-2 on penalties) Netherlands

France 2-1 Croatia

Third Place – Netherlands 2-1 Croatia

Some time after the event, the disgraced Fifa Official (at least he has a great name) Chuck Blazer admitted to taking bribes, along with other officials, for the awarding of the host status for this tournament. However, it turned out that the bribes had come not from France, but from a failed bid from Morocco.

It must have been doubly disappointing for the Africans if they did indeed commit the bribes – not only did they not get to host the event, but they lost their money as well.

France 98 saw a particularly unimportant addition to officiating. Rather than holding up a card to show injury time, electronic boards were first. Even less successfully, the golden goal was introduced, making teams even more cautious in extra time than they had been before. A mate of mine had a better answer than this nonsense. Have the penalty shoot out, then play the extra time. The penalties would only come into play if the score was still level after 120 minutes. The third innovation at this tournament was that three substitutions were permitted for the first time.

The final saw the mystery surrounding Brazil's star player, Ronaldo. Then, just before kickoff, he appeared on the pitch. Strange.

These started to count for more than the football

2002 – South Korea and Japan

Final – Brazil 2-0 Germany

Semi Finals – Brazil 1 – 0 Turkey

Germany 1-0 South Korea

Third Place – Turkey 3-2 South Korea

Although it was yet to reach Africa and Oceania doesn't even seem to be over the horizon, the 2002 World Cup at least showed that Fifa's reach was becoming a little more inclusive, with the first tournament to be hosted in Asia. Although by picking Japan and South Korea, it did not really meet its remit of including less advantaged countries of the world. It was also the only World Cup to date to be hosted by more than one country.

It was a tournament of surprises, and not just South Korea's remarkable run to the semi finals. France the holders and Argentina, second favourites, failed to make it past the group stage.

However, that succession of results by the joint hosts provoked some questions among those who believe that only the largest nations ought to win the trophy. It could almost be the Champions League, such was the determination that a great run by an unfancied team could be down to anything more than good play, tactical nous and hard work on their part.

Hosting the tournament so far away from Europe caused other problems to games great (ish) and good (ish). Time zone problems meant that games were played first thing in the morning, but schools and businesses adapted, opening late or, even more fun, showing games live before work started, often hiring big screens.

For many, the tournament happening so far away actually made it a more communal event than had it been in Germany or Spain.

But we cannot get far away from the controversy dreamt up around South Korea. Italy were furious about the ref's decision to send off Francesco Totti, and some have tried to make a link to that referee's subsequent prison sentence for drug trafficking.

And many claim that the two goals Spain scored in the quarter finals were legitimate although they were disallowed.

But that is not the fault of the South Korean players, and, let's face it, none of us are happy when our team loses – just think about Frank Lampard's disallowed strike against Germany in 2010, and how, had it stood, England would have gone on to win the World Cup. You don't hear the English going on about that, do you? No, although it was definitely a goal. Disgraceful refereeing. But we have let it pass, and moved on. As long as it never happens again. And that referee feels the guilt for the rest of his life.

The eventual winners, Brazil, were dominant without being spectacular. They won all of their matches, which is unusual, and set a new record for goal difference of +14.

The third place play off, featuring two unexpected teams (anybody who bet on that would have earned a good return), featured the fastest goal in World Cup history, with Hakan Sukur scoring in just 10.8 seconds.

But, for all the controversy, remarkable results and big screen joy, the tournament should best be remembered for Group F in the first round. It featured Argentina, England, Sweden and Nigeria and became the first, the original...'Group of Death!'

Thank goodness there has been one at every subsequent World Cup.

2006 - Germany

Final – Italy 1-1 (aet, 5-3 on penalties) France

Semi Finals – Germany 0-2 Italy

Portugal 0-1 Italy

Third Place – Germany 3-1 Portugal

In what is becoming an unpleasant habit, probably stemming from the corrupt behaviour at the top of Fifa until the removal from office of Sepp Blatter (we all hope that will move things forward), the German bid was surrounded with controversy.

It seems, by now, that under the table actions were not just taking place, but perhaps were even expected at the point at which hosts were appointed. Certainly, there were sudden commercial investments in countries whose football representatives had a vote. Football and politics separate beasts? If only.

Still, as the German Football Association President said in 2015, 'the World Cup was not bought' and he was able to 'absolutely and categorically rule out the existence of a slush fund.' The association backed up its statement by threatening to sue anybody who suggested anything different.

That's put that one to bed, then.

Although, we do know that genuine efforts to sway votes took place. A German magazine, rather like the English satirical rag, Private Eye, sent bribes to various officials, including promises of ham sandwiches made with genuine, Black Forest ham, if delegates would vote for Germany.

The finals saw the first occasion in which the defending Champions did not receive automatic entry into the competition.

Many of the stadia used for the tournament had to be renamed, because Fifa bans overt sponsorship unless by one of its official sponsors. So, what appeared to be a number of new grounds, such as the Fifa World Cup Stadium, were ones we knew by another. The example above is in fact the Allianz Stadium. An arena by any other name, will still smell as sweet.

Never let it be said that there could be any chance of financial hypocrisy when Fifa was in charge!

Another 'Battle of...' took place, with Valentin Ivanov, a Russian official, handing out no fewer than 16 yellow and four red cards in the Battle of Nuremberg, better known as the last sixteen match between the Netherlands and Portugal. Overall, the tournament set a new record for cards given out, with 345 yellow and 28 red. Graham Poll, the English referee famously gave three yellows to the same player, Josip Simunic, when Croatia played Australia.

Switzerland set two unfortunate records in the tournament. They were eliminated in the last sixteen, beaten by Ukraine in a penalty shoot-out. They missed all three of their spot kicks, to become the first team to miss every one of their attempts. They also went through the tournament without conceding a goal in normal play or extra time.

The final memorable moment came in the final itself, when Zinedine Zidane headbutted the Italian, Marco Materazzi. He was sent off.

2010 – South Africa

Final – Spain 1-0 Netherlands

Semi Finals – Uruguay 2-3 Netherlands

Germany 0-1 Spain

Third Place – Uruguay 2-3 Germany

Africa became the fifth continent to host the games. We now just need one to go to Australia, New Zealand, or the Cook Islands etc for the complete set. Having said that, given Fifa's normal record, Antarctica will probably get it first; at least there would be no problem with the weather being too hot, as might just be the case with Qatar in 2022.

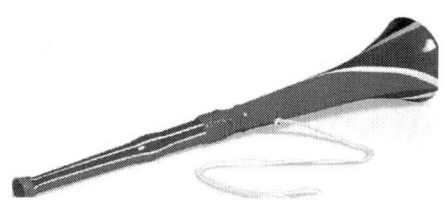

Ouch!

South Africa, though, set an unfortunate record, by becoming the only host nation to be eliminated in the first round. However, they were in good company. Both the winners and the runners up of the previous competition, Italy and France, were knocked out at this stage as well.

New Zealand were unlucky; the only team to be unbeaten in the competition, they were knocked out in the first stage as well.

Guess what? There was controversy – an understatement – over the awarding of the finals to South Africa. Allegations were made that the Fifa Vice President, Jack Warner, had been given $10 million to help secure the competition.

The story seems to have been confirmed by Chuck Blazer, who said that he, and others on the committee, had received money. Blazer is, as many will recall, the official who owned adjacent flats in an expensive complex, one for himself, the other for his cat.

Then, in 2015, a British newspaper reported that it had evidence that South Africa had not even won the vote to host the tournament – that had been Morocco – but South Africa got it anyway. Just think, we could all have been saved from death by vuvuzela.

An African team once again came close to reaching a World Cup semi final, when Ghana were awarded a penalty at the end of extra time against Uruguay. Luis Suarez had handled the ball on the line, stopping a certain goal, but the Ghanaians missed the penalty, and were eliminated in the shoot-out.

The final was refereed by England's Howard Webb and set a massive record for most yellow cards in a final, with 14.

2014 - Brazil

Final – Germany 1-0 Argentina

Semi Finals – Brazil 1-7 Germany

Argentina 0-0 (aet, 4-2 on penalties) Netherlands

Third Place – Brazil 0-3 Netherlands

The finals saw the introduction of goal line technology which, had it been available in 2010, would have seen England beat Germany thanks to Lampard's goal (no doubt) and, given three more goals and a couple of good results, win the cup.

Another first was the use of the referees' vanishing foam to mark free kicks and distances for walls.

Cooling breaks were also introduced because of the high temperatures and humidity levels. These were set for the thirty minute mark of each half where certain conditions were met. It is believed that they will last for the full 90 minutes in Qatar.

In an attempt to cash in on the 'success' of the vuvuzela, Brazil announced that the caxirola, a sort of clacker, would be their equivalent. Unfortunately, it was banned by all the grounds for safety reasons.

Given that this section is meant to highlight the odd, it is worth stating that there was no controversy surrounding the awarding of the finals to Brazil, with it being South America's turn and the only other applicants, Colombia, withdrawing early in the process. No controversy? That really is a shock.

To Save You Watching It, How Well Will The Teams Do?

Could it be?

Time for some fun. In the light of the draw, the potential of each team (as mentioned in the 'Prospects' sections for each team) might be compromised. Here is how the tournament is going to play out, so no stress, no arguing over the remote control, the tournament is decided. Have a go yourself, it's a great way to spend an hour. See below:

Group A

Uruguay 7 points (they draw with Russia)

Russia 5 points (a draw with Saudi Arabia; often the result of a tournament opener.)

Egypt 3 points

Saudi Arabia 1 point (downhill after the first match)

Group B

All decided on the second fixture, where Spain prove too strong for their neighbours.

Spain 9 points

Portugal 6 points

Morocco 1 point (a 0-0 and two 1-0 defeats)

Iran 1 point (hammered by the Europeans)

Group C

Very straightforward, this one.

France 9 points

Denmark 6 points

Peru 3 points

Australia 0 points

Group D

The fifth time in six competitions that Nigeria and Argentina have drawn each other. This is a group of shocks. Argentina's weakness is in defence, and it is going to cost them!

Nigeria 7 points (Victory over Argentina, a draw with Iceland)

Iceland 5 points (they defeat Croatia, plus two draws)

Argentina 4 points

Croatia 0 points

Could it happen?

Group E

An interesting group. Brazil should go through with ease, and Switzerland might just squeeze into second.

Brazil 9 points

Switzerland 4 points

Costa Rica 4 points (both beat Serbia, and draw against each other. But goal difference sways it, as Brazil get better and better through the tournament.)

Serbia 1 point

Group F

Another straightforward league. Germany too strong for all.

Germany 9 points

Sweden 6 points

Mexico 3 points (they have lost more World Cup games than any other team – two more in Russia)

Korea 0 points

Group G

It's going to come down to goal difference, and Belgium are more likely to score more regularly than England. England enter the last match knowing they need to win, because of goal difference, take the lead, try to sit back on it and Belgium get the equaliser.

Belgium 7 points

England 7 points

Panama 1 point

Tunisia 1 point

Group H

The weakest group, by a distance. Senegal triumph.

Senegal 7 points (a shock draw with Japan, but they still have enough)

Colombia 6 points

Poland 3 points

Japan 1 point

Last Sixteen

Uruguay v Portugal – Portugal just have enough legs to get through.

France v Iceland – An early goal from the tiny nation, and they almost hold on. It goes to extra time, then penalties, and that crowd makes the difference. Iceland triumph.

Brazil v Sweden – Brazil have too much class.

Belgium v Colombia – No question here, Belgium victorious.

Spain v Russia – Astonishingly, with decisions going their way, Russia triumph and interest in the competition continues.

Nigeria v Denmark – close, extra time and even penalties, but Africa has a representative in the quarter finals

Germany v Switzerland – Germany!

Senegal v England – it is closer than it should be, but England triumph, after extra time.

Quarter Finals

Portugal v Iceland – a match too far for the ageing Portuguese. Iceland pillage their way to the semi-finals.

Belgium v Brazil – goals fly in, nine in total. Game of all time, and the Belgium team is in the semi-finals.

Russia v Nigeria – good enough for Russia, and it is Nigeria in the semi-finals. 2-0.

England v Germany – the inevitable happens. 1-1 after 90 minutes, 2-2 after extra time, 5-3 on penalties – to England, every spot kick a goal.

Semi Finals

Iceland v Belgium – Despite their brilliant run, the skilful Belgians are too strong, and win by at least three goals.

England v Nigeria – England's best performance, they cruise to the finals by a margin of four.

3rd Place

Iceland triumph, an astonishing feat for such a tiny nation.

Final

Level after 90 minutes, the four goals split. England get a penalty, thanks to Raheem Sterling, score and hold on.

Actually, perhaps you'd better watch the tournament!

Injury Time – Last Words

Here we come to the end of our journey. Most probably, dear reader, you are from the Solomon Islands or Indonesia where, presumably spurred on by brief participation under the name of Dutch East Indies, your nations' interest in the World Cup has continued to thrive.

Forget Bobby Moore, Geoff Hurst et al, Pickles, the true hero of 1966

There are more Google searches for the term 'World Cup' in these nations than any other.

You are probably not American, because that was the least excited part of the world for the last tournament, and the US were taking part in that one.

But whether you are Indonesian, American, English, Russian or even Sepp Blatter, I thank you for buying my book and taking the time to get this far.

Let us hope that the 2018 finals thrill the world with roller coaster matches, end to end goals and the odd shock or two (as long as our own countries are not on the receiving end).

Let's hope that crowds are well behaved, racism and homophobic chants each go unheard and unseen, and that friendliness between nations is the overwhelming mood of the tournament.

Russia is the most wonderful of countries, and has its chance to show the world its welcoming nature, beauty and tolerance.

World Cup 2018 – here we come.

23847196R00150

Printed in Poland
by Amazon Fulfillment
Poland Sp. z o.o., Wrocław